To Melinda
One day at a time
Always Sherron

Experiencing
GOD
While
CAREGIVING

SHERRY NEWCUM

WESTBOW
PRESS®
A DIVISION OF THOMAS NELSON
& ZONDERVAN

WestBow Press books may be ordered through booksellers or by contacting:

WestBow Press
A Division of Thomas Nelson & Zondervan
1663 Liberty Drive
Bloomington, IN 47403
www.westbowpress.com
1 (866) 928-1240

ISBN: 978-1-5127-1100-4 (sc)
ISBN: 978-1-5127-1101-1 (hc)
ISBN: 978-1-5127-1099-1 (e)

Library of Congress Control Number: 2015914361

Print information available on the last page.

WestBow Press rev. date: 9/18/2015

CONTENTS

ACKNOWLEDGMENTS

To my husband, Bill Newcum—thank you for your constant encouragement and support ... even when I called you *Gene* because I had worked on my manuscript all day.

To my dear friends, Bev Hiatt and Kathy Brown. Kathy helped arrange my work schedule so I could work on this manuscript and corrected my medical lingo as needed. Bev encouraged me with her kind words and told me that it was helpful to her when she started to become a caregiver herself.

To my sisters, Donna and Lois. Donna Wagner was honest in her editing of my work and her encouragement. Lois Lindenfeld always believed in me when I didn't believe in myself and suggested I write down my thoughts and feelings through the whole process of caregiving and grief.

I also thank all the people who have prayed for me during this process—especially Angie Hernandez and Diane Pilcher, who kept me accountable.

Thank you all so much!

INTRODUCTION

When I was faced with the prospect of caregiving, I was not worried. I had worked in a nursing home and hospital and had plenty of caregiving experience. I didn't think about how caregiving could be exhausting when it was a 24/7 commitment, or that it can be lonely and emotionally draining at some points of the caregiving journey.

There were nurses and doctors I knew I could call when there was a problem. The list of specialists became more confusing than helpful; at one point, I called my husband's dentist begging for answers. He was the last doctor we had consulted, and I was desperate for answers concerning new changes in his health.

Doctors and specialists were great to talk to and ask questions. However, it wasn't like having someone in authority over me, as when I worked at the hospital. There someone else had the ultimate responsibility in my husband's care. Now the buck stopped with me.

I would soon find out I was over my head in care procedures. I would also soon find out that there was a definite time frame, and this time frame would end in the death of my husband. I was scared, but I was determined to make all our days together good ones. My husband's need for care and my flexibility continued in spite of my fears.

There was a time when my husband had a diet plan for his diabetes, a different one for his heart problems, and yet another one recommended for his kidney disease. At a clinic one month, I showed the nurse who was prepping him the three plans. On each plan, I had crossed out everything that was on the "not recommended" food list of the others. I said, "It looks like carrots are the only food he can eat."

It was frustrating juggling appointments, medications and medication changes, diet requirements, tests, supplies and therapy exchanges while trying hard to stay sane. I don't regret a minute of it as I look back, but there were plenty of times when I was tempted to throw in the towel and walk away.

A roller coaster of emotions, ragged nerves, and frustrations caused misunderstandings and hurt feelings for both my husband and me, adding negative feelings to the tasks at hand. With some creativity, I learned that the bad times can become good memories.

This book is not a comprehensive guide on caregiving. There are many manuals and books on caregiving. My husband happened to have kidney disease, which is very different from end-stage chronic obstructive pulmonary disease or Parkinson's disease or any other complex illness your loved one may have. Although you may not be going through the exact same processes, there are thoughts that may help you see your path with more clarity.

I hope this book will help you cope with those times when you are discouraged and feel like throwing in the towel but know you can't. My desire is that you will find strength within these pages and that this book will help some of the transitions you will face go more smoothly. Perhaps you will gain some insights into your own experience from reading the good and not-so-good ways I blundered through my experience.

The one driving reason I wanted to write this book is because I experienced something in the middle of caregiving that I had not experienced before. It has actually taken me five years to put my experience into words.

As quickly as my experience came, it also vanished—almost a year later to the day that my husband had entered the hospital for his last stay there. This book is about my experience of God's supernatural strength and clarity during a time of constant confusion and heartache. Now that I understand more about how God has worked in my life, I hope I can help you see and understand the process of transformation that may go on in your life as you read through my experience.

God kept revealing Himself to me in new ways and increasing my faith. At an early point in my journey through caregiving and grief, I fixed my eyes upon Jesus. Maybe that focus is like what occurred when Peter walked upon the water to Jesus. When he kept his eyes on Jesus, he experienced supernatural power to walk on water, when he turned his eyes from Jesus and focused on his surroundings, he sank in the water (Matthew 14:28–3). Sometimes, like me, you may feel forced out of your safe little boat and expected to do what you have never done before. As I recount my struggle and sway through caregiving, I hope you can get your sea legs too as you fix your eyes upon Jesus.

I have become a home healthcare worker since my husband's death. I have found that some of my insights are helpful to the families of my clients, who are doing their best for their loved ones. Sometimes we learn best by making mistakes; however, sometimes it is just as helpful to learn from another person's mistakes. You will question your efforts all through the process of caregiving and beyond: What would have been the best strategy? What would have been the best way to say this or handle that? Such doubts are normal. Each caregiving situation has its own trials. What worked for me may not work for you, but my hope is that my story and my knowledge will spark a creative way for you to handle your particular situation.

It comes down to the question, "Where do I start?" When I go to a mall, particularly one I have never been to before, I look for the directory. Once I find the map, I locate the red dot that says, "You are here." From there I can navigate through the maze of stores to find what I am seeking. I am hoping that you will be able to locate the red dot of your caregiving endeavor and identify your feelings and/or fears as you read about my experience and see the mistakes I made and the lessons I learned through my caregiving journey. I hope you will be able to navigate through your journey as a caregiver more easily and less fearfully to find what works best for you.

I am certainly not an expert; I am a sojourner. No one empathizes with your story like one who has been through something similar. Let's go on your journey together.

CHAPTER 1

Laying a Foundation

For the eyes of the Lord range throughout the whole earth to strengthen those whose hearts are fully committed to Him.

—2 Chronicles 16:9

Although the Lord gives you the bread of adversity and the water of affliction, your Teacher will be hidden no more, with your own eyes you will see the Teacher.

—Isaiah 30:20 ESV

So, we fix our eyes not on what is seen, but on what is unseen, since what is seen is temporary, but what is unseen is eternal.

—2 Corinthians 4:18

Acquiring eyes to see

I used to say, "My life was just a series of bad decisions." Then I had to learn to live with the consequences of those bad decisions, and that was not fun. I had had one failed marriage, and I was living in a marriage that was the result of another bad decision. In the midst of all my sorrow and pain, I learned to live with my eyes wide open. This realization was my first step in learning to trust God and God's promises.

God's promises are true. God promises to be with us. He promises to calm our fears. He even says, in Isaiah 41:13 ESV, "For I, the LORD your God, who takes hold of your right hand; it is I who say to you, 'Fear not, I am the one who helps you.'" Wow, it can't get better than that! God promises to take us by the hand and help us.

God's promises are based solely on God's character of love and compassion and other attributes. All God's other attributes, too numerous to include here, are intended for our good because God loves us and desires good for us. Why, then, do we experience so much suffering and so much confusion? That question would be a good topic for another book.

God's promises are not based on our desire, our attitude, or our performance on any level of service or behavior. God's promises are true whether we understand them or not. The truth of God's promises is a gift called *grace*. Grace is a gift from God. Grace is not based on us but on God's mercy, compassion, and love. Our part is the act of taking the gift, receiving it as our own, and allowing God to show us how He is working in us on our behalf.

When I said, "I learned to live with my eyes wide open," I was talking about receiving God's gift of grace that opened my eyes to

His reality. God gives us spiritual eyes to see His hand of caring help for us.

I know God's grace is free and true because I have seen it so many times. In fact, I have seen His grace at work protecting me and helping me and those I know so many times that I am totally convinced of His care.

Without doing a whole Bible study on God's grace, I cannot tell you if having my eyes opened to the work of God around me was spontaneous or something I had to request. Faith does not have to be based on a fairy tale or stories learned in Sunday school as a child. Sometimes those stories don't seem to make as much sense to us as we mature. Faith can be based on the testimony of others who have trusted God, received His gift of grace, and seen with their spiritual eyes God's reality. The stories in the Bible are true. However, as adults with the ability to understand events more abstractly than children can, we can see the stories in the Bible with adult depth rather than the simplicity of children.

In Hebrews 12:2, the Bible tells us we must "fix our eyes upon Jesus" because He is the author of our faith. We must "fix our eyes on what is unseen, not on what is seen, because what is seen is temporary and what is unseen is eternal," (2 Corinthians 4:18). The focus described in these Scriptures may sound like voodoo to someone who experiences this as a new concept.

We truly live by faith all the time. If we are living in or visiting a new city, we have faith that the road systems and signs are designed to get us to our destination safely. We don't stop to wonder if the directions provided are intentionally incorrect and follow our intuition. We trust the signs and/or the GPS to get us to our destination even if we encounter detours. With enough practice, we become familiar with the way to our destination, and we don't rely quite as much on the signs or the GPS.

Faith in God can be similar to the new directions scenario. We may not know how He works on our behalf, but we can find out by reading a Bible, talking to others who have experienced God, and attending to the testimony of ministers or other followers of Jesus. I know that I found that God cares for me and is involved with me. With enough experience, I learned to trust Him and His Word, even when life imposed some detours to my plans.

A Scripture that helped me was 2 Chronicles 16:9: "The eyes of the Lord range throughout the whole earth to strengthen those whose heart is fully committed to Him." It took me years to understand what this verse meant. I liked the idea that God was looking for me and would strengthen me when I needed it. Then one day I noticed that there was a qualifying statement at the end: "whose heart is fully committed to Him."

It took a few more years to figure out what that qualifier meant in my life. I ultimately had to ask God in prayer what having my heart fully committed to Him would be like. If you ask ten well-meaning people what a heart fully committed to God would be like, you would probably get ten different answers. People like rules and the predictability of cause and effect. So people are likelier to come up with rules or formulas for a life fully committed to God than they are to help you trust that God will help you learn to love and commit to Him.

God deals with us as individuals, and He is full of grace. He knows what makes you respond and what will drive you away. His desire is to draw you close and comfort you. For you or anyone else, living fully committed to God may have some aspects that are similar to those in my life. God has a plan for you, however, and it could look quite different from mine. It will look like something totally your own and within your authentic personality.

Growing through experience

The Scriptures above and the ways that God used them in my life prepared me for caregiving. It did take a lot of sorrow and pain in my life to get my spiritual eyes open, but that happened to me and has been very beneficial. Transformation in the midst of sorrow can happen to you, and your eyes will be opened to a different realm.

With my physical eyes, I could definitely see the sorrow; I felt the pain in the early years of my marriage. The pain and sorrow could take my entire focus and consume my day with useless hurt and struggle. Even on a beautiful day with friends or family, still I would be miserable.

It is easy for us to react to the visible realities in life, but there is so much more to see when we are open to seeing it. There is another way to see the pain and sorrow in our lives, and it is just as real and much less exhausting.

I couldn't have gotten through the three caregiving years that lay ahead of me had I not known that God's promises are true and that they are for me. If I had not been aware of God working in every situation for me and, more importantly, *with* me, I would have been as lost as any traveler in new territory without a GPS or a map. I would have felt the same fear I feel when I have to be at a very important event and am lost.

My eyes opened to see the spiritual reality through faith in Jesus Christ. I believed in Jesus as a person who walked this earth two thousand years ago, and I had faith in Jesus as the Son of God, Immanuel, and God with us. Jesus did not only give us practical examples of how to have a walking, working relationship with God while we are here on earth; He also accomplished for us what we could not do for ourselves.

Jesus made it possible for us to have a relationship with a perfect God by fulfilling the requirements of God and forgiving our sins. I believed and still believe, according to Hebrews 12:2, that Jesus was both example and provider of our ability to follow His example.

You have probably heard the term *born again*. It may have a bad connotation for you, though I hope it is a good connotation. Stay with me here. Dr. Richard D. Dobbins, a psychologist and pastor, puts it this way: "Being 'born again' does not mean 'trying harder' or 'turning over a new leaf.' It means that the part of you that is insensitive to God is made alive so that He can speak to you through your urges, your fantasies, and your ideas." I would add that *being born again* does not mean being obnoxious either.

In other words, being born again opens your heart and mind to God and his presence around you. To be born again, you only have to talk to God through prayer. This prayer should involve being honest and admitting you need help. Admit that you don't want anything to interfere with your ability to have His help, including sin. Confess that you have sinned and are ready to be forgiven, that you believe that Jesus died so that you may be forgiven, and that you want Jesus to be a part of your life. God will do the rest. You will have some struggles, but God is faithful and will help you. You will only have to ask Him for help.

I admitted, at the beginning of the prospect of caregiving that I could not face the years of caregiving without God. That was the attitude with which I started. That was my starting point: humbling myself and admitting I was weak and needed help, supernatural help from God. My years of unhappiness taught me I could rely on God when I needed him, and that taught me to be humble and to trust in God and His Son, Jesus.

Finding life

There is more that I want to share about my journey, and I hope this will help you in your journey. One day, a few years after Gene and I were married, he asked me a rather blunt question. It felt so out of the blue as we watched our boys swim at the beach. Since he was a workaholic, my casual schedule was less than endearing to him.

"What do you do?" he chided, with the suggestion that I contributed nothing to our existence.

Without any thought at all, I sang, "Stayin' alive, stayin' alive. Hoo, hoo, hoo, hoo, stayin' ali-i-i-i-ive," from the 1983 movie *Saturday Night Fever.*

Gene was quite irritated by my response, but for me, my spontaneous response was an eye-opening action. I thought to myself, "That is exactly what my life has become … just trying to stay alive and stay sane."

That is not the life Jesus died to give me, nor is it the life that He offers. So how are we supposed to live? Jesus says in John 10:10, "I have come that they may have life and have it to the full." Some translations say "have life in abundance." That was not my life, and I didn't know how to have a life of abundance. I didn't even know what that meant or what it would look like to live an abundant life.

I would have said, at that time, that the dominant characteristic of my life was numbness. *Numb and fighting for sanity* described me pretty well. That is probably a description of many young mothers' lives. I was aware that I was missing a lot in life, but I had no picture of what life to the full or in abundance looked like. I was definitely interested, though. My desire was to have life to the full or in abundance, whatever that meant.

Recently at a Beth Moore "Living Proof Live" event, I heard her talk about how she had gone through every reference in the Bible that mentioned "the joy" of Jesus, or complete joy. Joy is certainly a part of an abundant life, don't you think? She pointed out that her conclusion from reading all the references was that "complete joy" was always over something shared.

Jesus promises that, upon our belief in Him, that He, the Father, and the Holy Spirit come to live within us. In John 17:26, He actually prays that He may be in us. In Colossians 2:9–10, Paul tells the Colossians that all the fullness of the Godhead lives in Christ in bodily form. The triune life of Jesus is in the life of the believer, and the believer's life is in Him. Jesus desires to share life with us so that our lives will be abundant with His complete joy. This does not mean He will only be with us in the good times. He has promised never to leave us or forsake us. (Hebrews 13:5) No matter what we are going through, He will go through it with us.

Knowing that God is going through the tough times with us can give us strength to get through the tough times, even though we would sometimes like to give up. Finding joy in those tough times is a result of knowing there is someone who is bigger than our problem and knows the best way to get through it.

At some point I heard a message at a retreat or conference about looking for the lesson in our pain, and I started doing just that. I started praying for wisdom to see the lesson that God might have for me in the emotional strain I was suffering

I realize that many live with far worse consequences than I did. When we are feeling emotional pain, however, we are more focused on ourselves than on our surroundings until we give up the pain to choose life. We must be willing to give up our pain and open our eyes to see what life has to offer.

There is another step, but I don't know if this can happen without Jesus. Possibly we can see a lesson in our sorrow or pain, but I am not sure if the lesson we would see would be positive or negative.

In his book *Walking With God*, John Eldredge writes that sometimes we make agreements as results of negative lessons learned through life experiences; through these mental agreements with ourselves, we draw our own conclusion without God. For instance, some people who have lost a loved one, even though they prayed for recovery for that loved one, make an agreement. They may decide or make an agreement that God doesn't care about them, or even that God doesn't exist, when the loved one dies. This is not a healthy or positive agreement. Such agreements can last a lifetime unless honestly addressed with a pastor or trusted friend.

This is not a book on how we make agreements or get ourselves into messes of our own making. At this point, you may wonder what any of this has to do with caregiving and what this book *is* about.

CHAPTER 2

Finding My Attitude

Do everything without complaining or arguing, so that you may become blameless and pure, children of God without fault in a crooked and depraved generation.

—Philippians 2:14, 15

But he said to me, "My grace is sufficient for you, for my power is made perfect in weakness."

—2 Corinthians 12:9

Attitude makes the difference in how we see reality. Attitude is a choice and helps us elect to get stronger in the midst of our personal crises or to become a victim of them.

The point I am trying to make is that there is an attitude that needs to be acquired, and that attitude needs to be positive.

Finding my attitude

Most people have heard that attitude is everything. That is true, but not all attitudes are good or positive. I think the best attitude for any new venture is an attitude of expectancy. It is easy to have an attitude of "Why me?" or "I just can't take it anymore," or "Poor me." No one would blame you for having any of those attitudes as you face the prospect of caregiving. But there is empowerment in the right attitude, one that finds strength in weakness and beauty in the midst of tragedy. I believe this attitude is a gift of God.

With the right attitude, we stay resilient when everything around us seems to be against us. A good attitude holds onto hope when the life we dreamed of appears out of reach. Expecting a life lesson that will strengthen us is hugely important when we feel worn out or anxious. Expecting to see God revealed to us in a new way is exciting in the midst of burdens.

If you don't know how faithful God is, then you are in for an adventure. If you do know that God is faithful, the realization that he is also personally faithful in the midst of our struggles will be a comfort.

An attitude of expectancy or even curiosity opens our eyes to see the unexpected. I don't know how it works, but I have experienced it and have heard others talk about it. I guess it is something like when you buy a new car and think you are the only one who has a car like that. Then, when you are out driving, you see a lot of cars like yours. Something shifts in the way we see other cars. Something can shift in how we see life. For me, having faith that God would not leave me alone on this journey helped me to see the many ways He was involved.

Expect the unexpected

Desire to see God working on your behalf—even if, at this point, you don't have strong faith in God. He is here, and He is just waiting for us to open our eyes to His dimension so we can see Him at work on our behalf. There is no risk involved, and you may find the treasure of God's help in the midst of your trials. Stronger faith and trust will come later if we just stay open to the idea that God cares enough to become involved with us.

Watching helplessly as someone we love suffers has a way of making us open our minds to the idea of needing help from one bigger than ourselves, whether we want to admit it is God or not. When we are watching someone we love suffer, we realize that we do not have an ounce of control to change the situation. We don't like feeling helpless. When our spouse or parent or child who was always so strong, healthy, and happy becomes helpless and totally dependent on us to help them, we feel even more helpless. We want to think we can handle it and that we have what it takes to do a good job, but all of us may not have that confidence.

Of course we assume that we know what is best for the situation and the one we love. More than anything, we want our loved one to be healthy.

We hope that, by working together, we can get back to the life we planned. We are intent on solving the problem before us. We can read up on the illness of our loved one, and we can prepare ourselves for the journey ahead. At some point, though, we will know we have no control.

Maybe, at that low point in our life, when we feel helpless and hopeless, we are willing to admit that we need God, but we want to be in control of him. We want him to follow our orders. Our prayers are full of demands and complaints, and we desire control over our situations and God, our puppet. We want to pull certain strings and have God move in the direction of our pull. God doesn't expect us to be His puppets, and we need to get over the tendency to think that He is ours.

The opposite of control is trust. We should trust God, but even if we don't trust Him, He is faithful. He will teach us to trust Him.

God is love, and there are many ways He shows His love. As parents, we know that the best thing for our children is not always what they want. We also know that sometimes children will settle for something that interests them for the moment. We know there is something far more exciting, or at least better, in the near future for them; they just don't know it yet. God's love also doesn't mean that we will get everything we want just because we ask for it. Sometimes God has something in mind that is far better for us than we can imagine at the moment we are praying.

That seems harsh to say when you may be watching someone you love so much waste away. I know that; I have been there. After weeks of my husband's intense suffering, I felt no real answer to my sincere and heartfelt prayers. To make our situation worse, we were told that there was no hope for his full recovery. The best we could hope for was another year in a nursing home with the aides, "Susie and Paula" repositioning him at scheduled times. The day Gene was buried, I couldn't imagine there was more life for me—abundant or not.

My first step in forming a good attitude was being open to the idea that God would be intimately involved with me and with Gene. I was convinced that, because of God's past involvement with me, we would see Him working on our behalf.

The next step for me was deciding to have an attitude of expectancy and wonder. It is easy, when we feel out of control, to try all the harder to take control. Our focus becomes our own efforts. At some point, I must have given up on all my own efforts and just given over the situation to God. I had a sense of expectancy that caused wonder at the miracles, great and small, that we would encounter. I expected God's love to be revealed to me in newer ways than I had experienced before.

At the very beginning of our journey, we both had an attitude of fear. It is normal to have fear in the face of a new situation. I had to make a decision to rise above my attitude of fear and remember that God says, "Fear not," or something similar, three hundred and sixty-five times in the Bible. That is one time for every day of the year. It sounds like a command, but it comes with a promise of God's presence with us. We can rely on that promise, but we have to make a decision to "fix our eyes"—to focus on what God is doing for us. At some point I took my focus off my own efforts. I never stopped trying to make Gene's life the best it could be, but the fear that it all depended on me was gone.

CHAPTER 3

Let the Games Begin

Let your eyes look straight ahead; fix your gaze
directly before you.

—Proverbs 4:25

"For I know the plans I have for you," declares the
Lord, "plans to prosper you and not to harm you,
plans to give you a hope and a future."

—Jeremiah 29:11 NIV

As I wrote earlier, my husband was a workaholic. His work always
came first. It was more important than his personal care and health,
and it was more important than his relationships. It's not uncommon,
but it is deadly. For my husband, his need for future caregiving was
predictable because of his health habits, but the reality of it did not
set in for us until later.

His doctor had been telling him, since his diagnosis of Type II
diabetes, that he needed to watch his carbohydrate intake, exercise,

and control his portion sizes. Later, in his fifties, the doctor and nurses tried to explain how hard it was on his kidneys to have high blood sugar continually. Later, in his seventies, his doctor sympathized with him.

He said, "I know taking care of yourself seems like an inconvenience." Then he imitated an elderly man wheeling himself by kicking his feet one at a time, hunched over in his wheelchair, down a nursing home corridor. "But this is even more inconvenient, and this is your fast-approaching future if you don't start helping yourself by following our instructions."

Nonetheless, we sat stunned a year or so later when his doctor told us that his kidneys were, in fact, failing. He was at 30 percent of his kidneys' ability to function. When his kidneys were between 10–15 percent of their function, he would need to start dialysis.

It, whatever health diagnosis you are ignoring, can happen. Those misfortunes that we think will never happen to us, only to others, can happen. We were not exempt from the predictions. Also, our doctor said that our hospital would not accept Gene's insurance and had no dialysis unit. We would have to find a new doctor, one associated with another hospital near us that would accept Gene's insurance and had access to a dialysis center and lab.

At that moment, we had no idea what was ahead for us. Our future was a blank page. Like everyone, we planned a retirement that included some traveling, spending some fun times with our grandchildren, and some relaxing times enjoying life, but we were not sure if any of that would be our retirement plans now.

Game on: learning to cope

The next morning, I had gone down to start the coffee when I heard a thud on the floor above me—where our bedroom was. I ran upstairs to see if Gene was okay. He was pulling himself up from the floor. He said he was very dizzy. As he started to walk, he fell again.

"Please lie down on the bed," I pleaded. "I will call Greg and see if he can come and help you walk down the steps. I am afraid if I help you and you fall, we will both go down the hard way."

Greg was his son; Greg worked from his home and had a somewhat free schedule. He also was a first responder for his local fire department. I felt God had blessed us by providing for this need, and I thanked Him. Greg came immediately and helped Gene walk safely down the steps. He said that it seemed like vertigo, but that we should take him to the doctor to find out. We went to our normal doctor because we hadn't had time to look for a new one.

The doctor told us that if we went to the ER at the new hospital, Gene would be assigned a doctor who would take his case. He sent us to the ER with Gene's medical history and a recommendation that he be admitted to the hospital, specifying why he could no longer take Gene as a patient. The vertigo was mild, but God was helping us with our future need for a doctor.

We walked out the door with no real plan other than what the moment called for. It all seemed mechanical, and we did not want to look ahead. *Mechanical* seemed the most comforting mode, and this moment seemed all that existed. As unsure as we were, I was glad that this vertigo was as minor as it was and that it would provide a way to be involved with another doctor and hospital. I think the episode was a blessing in disguise.

Fortunately, Greg could continue with us to the hospital and drive us there. I was numb, and life was surreal. When our health is good, we think we are indestructible, so when life catches up with us, shock and grief set in. Grief is associated with loss, and loss of the life we had dreamed of seemed imminent.

Gene knew his life was changing, and not for the better. I could see the sadness in his eyes. Of course, we still hoped our doctor was wrong. We still believed we could make a change and beat the odds. I know it was unrealistic to have such a belief, but hope often runs deep. We needed hope. We needed the strength that hope provides to go on and the peace it can give to settle our spirits.

Develop a design

It's funny what went through my mind as the blurry world passed by our car window. I remembered my garden. I had a beautiful perennial sitting garden at our house. About ten years earlier, it had been a problem part of our yard. We had tall walnut trees and other trees that shaded the yard. Grass grew there very sparingly, but weeds grew there quite well and overtook the grass. Oddly enough, the flowers that I planted in a flower bed flourished. I decided to till up that whole area of my yard, take a chance that flowers would flourish, and make a perennial sitting garden.

I started by digging an area to set some landscaping blocks to build a place to set a table and chairs, then I tilled all the way around it and tilled the whole area that had very little grass. Actually, my eighty-nine-year-old father did the tilling. I remembered sitting on a chair in the middle of the barren, tilled ground and crying. I was crying because I had no idea what I was going to do with it. I had no plan.

Dad had worked harder than he should have, and I didn't even know what I was going to do with it. I was afraid it would be just another failure, and this whole project would be just another bad decision. Looking at my yard as a reality with no plan rather than a dream made me feel overwhelmed, and I bawled. I put my head in my hands and bawled until I was worn out.

Remembering that time in my life, as we drove into our unknown future, made me think. I did not feel up to the challenge of a garden, a job, and being a wife and mother at that time. Remembering that day as we were driving to the hospital reminded me of how I had felt overwhelmed then, but my project had worked out. Our future was like a gray, barren place with no plan. Right at that moment, while riding in the car, I was wondering if I was up to the task of caring for Gene and everything else in our life.

Gene's health, of course, was far more important than how to shape a garden. The fear was more intense, the risk far greater, but I had been in this spot before. It wasn't totally unfamiliar, and yet the weightiness of our present situation was new.

I remembered walking away from the blank, tilled soil and not looking back. The next morning I looked out the window from my desk and there it was … the same gray soil with clumps of tilled grass and random footprints. A week went by, and I did nothing. Two weeks passed. Then weeds started emerging.

I bought some plants and some shrubs to define the borders of the garden. The garden was like a jigsaw puzzle; I decided that if I could get a border, the rest of my design would happen later. I decided I couldn't add failure to my hope of a garden. Without a plan, my garden could turn into a nightmare, and so could this new adventure of caregiving.

I had to make the same kind of determined decision now about this whole turn of events with Gene. By the time we reached the hospital ER, I had gained some resolve. Although our future seemed much like a barren, tilled garden, it was our future, from which we would now design something beautiful within our new set boundaries. We could do it with some work and determination. Maybe, like the garden, our future would all work out.

I realize, now that I have been through the caregiving process, that caregiving is a matter of design. Sometimes, as we go through the experience, we must make some plans. Sometimes we are blessed to have the help of others so that we can make a plan.

With my garden, it was a matter of adding plants that would bloom according to the exposure to light or shade. I wanted something blooming all the time, and that would mean choosing and planning the plants I bought. I wanted there to be a place of peace to sit among the flowers as they bloomed. In my garden I had an area I kept wild. I planted woodland plants and placed some interesting logs to add a feeling of a wild forest. I would add borders to my garden to make its distinctness from the rest of the yard more observable. I could see, as I rode along in the car, that my caregiving efforts could have similar aspects. It would be best done by design and not left to chance.

Our journey through his illness would present its own borders from the life we had dreamed of, but it would have its own uniqueness. I did not know, as I was designing and planting the garden, that Gene would find the comfort and peace he needed through prayer in the years ahead while sitting in that very garden. He would spend whole afternoons sitting in the swing, head bowed and hands folded. Wait—maybe he was sleeping! Either way, it was his haven. It was his connection with peace and God that he needed.

Perhaps you are not a gardener or a designer, but you find yourself in the same sort of dilemma: an unknown journey into failing health. You are faced with a blank future of caregiving. You feel overwhelmed and wonder if you are up to the task. You are aware you are on an emotional roller coaster, realizing you must juggle your own insecurity, your loved one's fears, and perhaps a job and family. It is a lonely feeling, and if you put too much thought into it, you may feel paralyzed. There isn't time for self-pity. Like me, you may, at times, wonder if you will ever get the luxury of feeling sorry for yourself or even just caring for yourself again.

The benefit of having gone through caregiving is that I learned a few techniques. Experience is an amazing teacher, especially if you make a lot of mistakes. I surely did. I'm not an expert; I'm a sojourner. The journey, the emotional roller coaster, the designing is familiar territory, but each journey is its own. I discovered a few experiences that I think are common to many caregivers of a loved one. The roller coaster of highs and lows goes faster than we think we can handle, and some of the designing happens without our input. Sometimes we have to adjust our plans and stay far more flexible with our time than seems fair.

The best strategy in a new situation is to take it one day at a time. If we start with speculation and let the "what ifs" flow out of control, we can get a little nuts. Maybe that is why God tells us, in Proverbs, to "let our eyes look straight ahead," to stay in the moment and fix our gaze upon Him.

CHAPTER 4

Facing the Facts

The Lord is close to the brokenhearted and saves
those who are crushed in spirit.

—Psalm 34:18

So do not fear for I am with you; do not be dismayed,
for I am your God. I will strengthen you and help
you; I will uphold you with my righteous right hand.

—Isaiah 41:10

At first, when we hear that a loved one is ill, we are determined.
We made a vow once, if we are married, before God. We said, "in
sickness and in health," and we meant it. Now we will live that
vow out. It's normal to feel such determination and love, and it is
admirable. For others, we know it is the right thing to do and we
must do it, which is also very admirable. The journey may seem long
and beyond our strength, but there is still that sense that we promised
and that we care.

Gene told me, as his health started to deteriorate, that if I wanted to get out of the marriage, I could get out. It wasn't so much that I didn't want to, since I feared what was ahead, as that I couldn't. I absolutely could not leave him when he was probably going to need me more than ever before. I had no idea how totally dependent on me he would become, and I don't regret a minute. I think they should add a vow, though, that says, "If I am the one who is sick, I promise to be appreciative of my spouse."

Another taste of grief

A sort of grief sets in when we are faced with the life change that a terminal illness can bring. It affects the whole family as we face shattering dreams. For the caregiver, it can feel like a yoke of constant appointments and responsibility that person never asked to bear. For the one who is ill, there is grief over the inevitable end of life as he knew it and before he is ready. The first step in grief is anger. Although the one who is ill is not angry with the caregiver, the caregiver is the one who is there. The caregiver usually gets the brunt of that frustration and impatience on top of the caregiver's own feelings of frustration and resentment. Whew! Take a deep breath!

Gene's health started to deteriorate in obvious ways. He became legally blind from high blood sugar levels that damaged the blood vessels in his eyes. He had many laser surgeries until his doctor told us he had done all he could do. Because of his poor vision, Gene lost his driver's license and his independence. He developed what we would later discover was arthritis in his neck, and it was hard for him to hold his head up or keep his balance when he walked.

Losing his independence was probably one of the hardest challenges for him when it happened. After talking to a few people,

I think losing a driver's license is hard for many. I wonder if it is partly that those who have their license taken away have to admit they are getting old. We all know we are getting older, of course, but we often think we are much younger than we actually are. Aches and pains can be joked about or written off as the result of using muscles we haven't used for a while, but having to give up a driver's license is a sure sign that life is not what it once was. I am probably trying to be too empathetic, but I know that once Gene lost his license and felt stuck at home, he became very irritable. In trying to be kind to him, my actions were taken as condescension or as treating him like a child ... or an elderly person.

Denial

I did chalk up some of the health problems going on with Gene to old age and didn't really worry about them. One time at church, Gene was having trouble holding his head up. He put his arms on the pew in front of him and laid his head on his arms. At this point, we were unaware that he had arthritis, and he said he was just more comfortable when he laid his head down for just a little while. A nurse several pews back saw him and came over during the worship service to see if we needed help. She thought that he had gotten light-headed or was in pain. He assured her that he was fine, that this was normal, and that he was handling it.

She said, "This is not normal, and I recommend you go talk to a doctor about it."

We did make an appointment with our doctor, and he did not see any reason for Gene's inability to hold his head up. Gene did not want a CT scan.

Gene heard about a health product on the radio that promised great results. Which ones don't? He called the number, and we met with a couple who were selling the product. She had had amazing results with her hyperthyroid problem, and her husband was in a wheelchair, but he was very strong. They gave us phone numbers of people we could call and get testimonials, including men who had been helped with kidney disease. We did call, and we were able to ask questions about how this product might help Gene.

We decided to buy the product and become distributors. We both got fantastic results, and we were very happy. Gene had started noticing that he felt so much better and stronger. The next time we went to the doctor, his kidney function was increasing. Although the increase was slight, he was glad to have any improvement. The doctor did not say anything about putting in the port he had told us about at the last appointment. We were ecstatic!

Now we had a real testimony with our new business that people would want to hear and, best of all, a new hope. Gene was a hero at our weekly meetings, and we were getting phone calls from people all over the country who wanted to hear his testimony. These developments were looking very good for us. He just had one problem, and that was constipation.

A day before we were supposed to go to a conference, Gene had an appointment with his new doctor. His doctor was out of town, but he had a substitute. Gene told the substitute doctor that mostly he was okay, but he had this problem with constipation, and his balance was a little off. She started telling him about herself and that she had done her residency with an ear, nose, and throat specialist. She thought maybe some of his balance problem could be problems with his ears. She noticed they were very waxy and started cleaning them out. She was cleaning his ears, and he was talking about constipation.

The whole scene seemed a little odd to me. When she thought she had done all she could do that day for his ears, which we didn't even know were a problem, she offered him some free samples of a new drug for constipation. He took them as prescribed.

When we got home, he started the recommended dosage, two pills in the evening and two pills in the morning. The next morning we took off for our conference in Chicago.

Since Gene could not drive or read, we had this little deal when we traveled that I would do all the driving and check us into the hotel, and he would bring the luggage. When we got to the conference center, I found a parking spot and went into the hotel. When I was done checking us into the hotel and conference, there was still no Gene. I went out to the parking lot and found Gene there, carrying the luggage, not very far from the car. I was a little irritated and hurried out toward him. Then I noticed he was winded and really struggling. I grabbed the suitcase and his arm, and we walked into the lobby and found a seat.

"What's going on? I asked.

"I'm just so weak. I was light-headed when I got out of the car, so I sat down for a while. When I tried again I was not light-headed, but I was still weak. I had a really hard time getting the luggage out of the car. I think I want to skip the meeting tonight and just lie down in the room."

"Of course. Can you walk to the room?"

We managed to get him to the room, and he lay down immediately. I went to the meeting alone and was not worried. At this point we just thought he needed a good rest because the ride had been too much. Everyone was disappointed that he could not attend; they wanted to hear his story and ask some questions. In the morning he was better. He wasn't really strong, but he was better. We met some friends for breakfast and went on to the meeting. Part of the way through the morning session, Gene started to get weak again, and I helped him to our room.

On the way home from the conference, I said that I thought what was going on with him sounded like it could be side effects.

When we got home, I checked the information sheet and he did, in fact, have every single side effect. In fine print at the bottom, it said, "No tests have been done on patients with kidney loss." We had trusted the doctor even though she seemed more interested in his ears than anything else, and we had the conference on our minds. I felt horrible that I had not checked the side effects sooner. He was so weak that I took him to the hospital, and they admitted him. I told the ER doctor that Gene was seeing a nephrologist, and they called his doctor. He ordered a test to check his creatinine level. It was very high, and the nephrologist sent him to surgery to put in a temporary port so they could do emergency dialysis.

Facing the truth

We were very disappointed, and the same numbness we had felt when his former doctor told us we needed to look for a new doctor came over me. The same blank page came to mind. Our lives had seemed to be on a page of hope for recovery, where Gene was a hero with real hope of getting progressively better and we were working together in business. Now, with Gene starting dialysis, our life seemed to be a blank page again.

This was the beginning of the roller coaster we could not leave. Life would be a series of ups and downs: highs and lows we could not control. I'm sure I just stared at the floor during the surgery while they put in his port. The doctors wanted to wait until the next morning to do his dialysis to make sure his body did not reject the port. I spent the night at the hospital with Gene.

I wish I loved to Google everything. That would have been so helpful. At least I would be able to know what questions to ask the doctor. His comments to me might have made more sense. Then, in turn, I could have helped Gene through all his care a little more easily. Maybe, if he had actually understood his situation, he would have been more willing to work with the doctors and trust their diagnosis. As it was, this whole situation was very disappointing for him and made him angry.

A nurse told me that paranoia is a symptom of sleep deprivation. His workaholic lifestyle caused him to function daily on two to four hours of sleep, and he sometimes went without any sleep at all for forty-eight hours. His response to the whole situation was to say that the doctors were just trying to collect on his insurance and that he was fine. I told him I wished that were true, but the doctor seemed to know what he was talking about, and I thought he had Gene's interest at heart.

He stayed one more night after he had his first dialysis, and then we went home. He had an appointment to have dialysis three times a week at a dialysis center near us. The only available time was at 6:30 AM Tuesday, Thursday, and Saturday. Our weekly business meetings were on Saturday, an hour away from the dialysis center. The hospital where Gene had had his emergency dialysis was right across the street from where we had our meetings. I thought that if we could do his Saturday treatment at the hospital, I would not have to find someone to take him to his Saturday appointments while I went to the meetings, which were required. There was no opening there or anywhere else in that city. That's when I realized how epidemic kidney failure must be. There were about four hundred thousand Americans on dialysis in 2006.

It was a rare occasion when Gene followed his doctor's advice for more than a few days. He was locked into the dialysis appointments; the alternative was death. He would go, but he would let me know all the way there how much he resented it. Fortunately, the nephrologist and nurse practitioner were very happy people, and Gene connected with them. A young nurse with problems of her own because of a severe car accident was a positive influence. He really listened to them. I felt comfortable leaving him there and going to a nearby bagel and coffee shop for the duration of his treatment each time.

While I had coffee, I wrote in a journal. I just wrote from my heart, expressing my fears and my inadequacy. I didn't know how to pray about our future, and I didn't know how my faith would play into this. Was my faith enough to move this mountain? In Matthew 17:20, the Bible promises that if we have faith only the size of a mustard seed (very tiny) and believe, we can move mountains. It was at that moment that I asked Jesus into our situation. I knew I needed God's help, wisdom, and clarity.

I had been through years of Bible study and recalled a phrase from Exodus 33. "If your Presence does not go with me, I don't know what I will do," I wrote in my journal. My prayer was sincere, and I needed the peace that passes understanding, which the Scriptures promise.

Getting the scoop

In our church there was a woman whose husband had been on dialysis until he died. She overheard me talking about Gene's dialysis to a friend. She came over and asked me to follow her. When we were where no one else could hear, she said, "This will be hard for you to hear, but if Gene has started on dialysis, he probably only has about three years to live. I worked full time as a nurse …"

I had stopped listening to let the words "three years to live" soak in. What did that mean? Three years? Literally three years? Or just three good years before he would become ill? My mind was racing. I was sure she meant well, and I was sure our experience would be different from her experience. We would have forever.

She continued, "If I could do it all over again, I would have quit my job and spent those last three years with my husband."

She was a nurse and had been through this exact journey we were about to start. As much as I wanted to dismiss what she said, seeds of thought were planted, and our future started to take shape. Now the thought of being alone in only three years added a new blank page. How would we live through the next three years without either one of us having a real job? My concern for the future changed from "How am I going to get us through this?" I added, "And how will I go on when this is all over?"

So many thoughts were going through my head as she continued telling me stories of her own experience. I heard very little. I heard something about needing to move their bedroom downstairs as her husband became weaker. Where would we put our bedroom if we had to move it downstairs?

"No one dies because they are on dialysis," I heard her say, "but when the kidneys stop functioning, everything in the body gets out of balance." The impact of this simple statement would be lost to me in my mental ramblings.

I told Gene what she had said when I got home, but I think he must have let the words fly by without letting them soak in. His response was his usual response to anything he didn't want to hear: "I have work to do."

At the dialysis center, they set up a time for us to talk to the nephrologist. The temporary port they had put in needed to be removed because of possible infection. We would have to make another decision on a matter about which we knew nothing. The doctor told us about peritoneal dialysis that Gene could do at home. If we were interested, they would set up a time for us to see a video about it and some testimonials from patients who had switched from hemodialysis to peritoneal dialysis.

Hemodialysis was the kind of dialysis done at a center. Hemodialysis mechanically cleanses the blood outside the body to remove various substances that would normally be removed by the kidneys and then returns the blood to the body. Peritoneal dialysis is a technique that uses the patient's own body tissues inside the abdominal cavity as a filter. The method of dialysis he chose would determine where the permanent port would be surgically implanted.

We were told that peritoneal dialysis would allow us more freedom and be more convenient. The video was very convincing. Talking to my friend, we found that it was fairly easy and did indeed provide more freedom. Since this treatment was done three times a day every day, it was more like his kidneys would normally function. Since we live in northern Indiana, our appointments would be before the snowplows were out on the snowy mornings of winter. It would be too inconvenient to continue treatment at the dialysis center thirty minutes away. Doing peritoneal dialysis at home was the best idea.

Just a note: If you and your loved one are facing dialysis, doing peritoneal dialysis at home is not hard, and the medical service providers have continuous ambulatory peritoneal dialysis (CAPD) nurses on call 24/7. We found the nurses very helpful and compassionate, but this treatment is a lot of responsibility. Since there are nearly four hundred thousand people on dialysis in this country, there is a great chance that someone reading this book will be facing this same decision: hemodialysis or peritoneal dialysis. I hope this description of our thinking is helpful to you.

He was not supposed to eat before he started his hemodialysis; by the time it was over, his blood sugar had dropped, making him very weak. Gene was usually so weak after his treatments that he could hardly walk out to the car from the center because his sugar level was so low. Many times, he fell before we got to the car; we finally faced the fact that he needed a wheelchair every time he had hemodialysis.

Stay grounded. Ask questions.

I recommend asking as many questions as you can and fully understanding both types of dialysis. Journaling is a great way to get to the questions for which you need answers. Writing your queries out slows down your thinking process, which usually goes faster and more randomly than the hand can write. Journaling helps us stay focused on the issue at hand and look methodically at the situation.

Often our imaginations make up some really crazy scenarios that can seem quite possible with only casual thought. Slowing the thought process down contributes to seeing our imaginings as just fantasies. Changing health has its own monsters to battle without speculation adding more monsters that don't need to be there. Our imaginations may still run wild, but we can lasso them like wild horses and bring them into the corral for a closer, realistic look through journaling.

If you are from the era of Alfred Hitchcock, you have an idea where unrestrained imagination can take us. For a movie or a book, let imagination run wild, but when dealing with real life—journal. A journal was also good for referring back to when life seemed overwhelming and I had forgotten why I made a certain decision.

A few people I talked to told me their husbands had chosen peritoneal dialysis and that it did, in fact, allow more freedom, and that they felt better. Gene was all about freedom, and who doesn't want to feel better? So the decision was made, and we went for training.

*I got the dialysis numbers from the WebMD

A Winter Garden

Stalks of flowers
Now dead and brown
Stand tall
Above the snow.
They speak of life
And how it was
Not so long ago.

CHAPTER 5

Fulfilling a Purpose A Winter Garden

Stalks of flowers
Now dead and brown
Stand tall
Above the snow.
They speak of life
And how it was
Not so long ago.

I praise you because I am fearfully and wonderfully made; your works are wonderful, I know that full well.

—Psalm 139:14

The body is a unit, though it is made of many parts; and though all its parts are many, they form one body. So it is with Christ.

—1 Corinthians 12:12

The kidneys are small organs that are tucked into the back under the ribs. They are about the size of a fist and have a million units called nephrons, which filter the blood. All the blood in the body passes through the kidneys several times a day. The kidneys regulate the blood's acidity and mineral balance, among other important functions. They are the body's master chemists. When they are not doing their job, other organs pick up the slack, but not as well as the kidneys. The body's pH can become imbalanced, and other organs try to compensate by secreting their own version of the minerals or hormones needed. This description is an oversimplification, but this text is not a medical journal.

We are the church.

When the kidneys are not doing their job, less-qualified organs try to pick up the slack. They do their best, but this compensation mechanism actually causes more problems. One day we were learning about the function of the kidneys and that we have organs about which we had never heard. I thought that this process was much like the church.

There are people who have definite gifts to fulfill functions in the church. When they do not make productive use of the talents God has granted them through the body of Christ, the church suffers. There can be many reasons why people are unable to use their gifts within the church, and most have to do with spiritual or emotional health.

Maybe a person doesn't know his or her gift or doesn't have the confidence to use that gift if that person has low self-esteem or does not know the power of the Holy Spirit within the self. Sometimes we are too lazy or too busy to make a commitment. Perhaps this person is a caregiver for another person and has limited free time. Sometimes we don't like our gifts and are jealous of someone else's gift.

There are many reasons for not using our gifts, but whatever the reason, the body of Christ suffers from a lack of functioning parts. Each person is needed. The kidneys are needed, and when they cannot do their job anymore, the body suffers. The liver and the parathyroid try to do the job of the kidneys, but the result is not the same. They become overworked; they are less effective than the kidneys. Now their functions, as well as kidney function, have been compromised.

When we are well physically, we hardly ever think about any of our physical functions. We feel good and move easily and painlessly. We have energy and the ability to do whatever we want, but when any part of us becomes painful or does not function well, we have to change our activities or the way we accomplish things. We become less effective in our world, and we are not happy. That is why Paul uses this illustration in 1 Corinthians, I think. We all know how we feel when some part of our physical body is not working as it should.

I know that I am less aware of how the body of Christ feels when I am not doing my part, but the body still suffers. There is still some poor person who is trying to do the job God has gifted me to do. This person does not have my gift and is tired from trying to do too much. The body of Christ is not as effective as it could be. There are many different functions in the body of Christ. Not all of them are prominent roles. Just as many times our hands may be doing small tasks, the hand is still very important. I would guess there is no part of your body you would want to live without. All parts of the body of Christ are important to Him and are needed. I felt a definite call by

God to knit sweaters for kids. That seems quite small as we consider the needs, function and outreach ministries of the church, but it has proved to be quite needed and I rarely have to leave home to fulfill this gift and ministry God has given me.

I do not want anyone to feel guilty about not using personal gifts in the church if life's responsibilities seem overwhelming. As the Book of Ecclesiastes says, "There is a time for everything."

If you feel you would like to still contribute to the church, there are ways. One woman in our church who was caring for her grandson with fourth-stage cancer made simple blankets for other cancer patients in our church. She arranged for people to pray for that person at certain times of the day. The recipients were to put the blankets on their laps during those periods of time and allow the prayers to cover their concerns. She hosted a Bible study in her home weekly. Guess who was first on our prayer list each week!

Some women make prayer shawls, have their pastor bless them, and take them to others. If we ask how we can be of service to God, ideas will come in some way. If the thought of doing something more than your daily schedule is overwhelming, that is not a problem. Your responsibilities are enough.

We pray for ourselves when we are sick, and our prayer lists at church are filled with need for physical healing. Only speaking for myself, I have never given a thought to healing for the body of Christ. I think that if the job is getting done, that is all that is required. I guess I think that if the body is limping forward, it is moving forward, and that is all that is essential. I don't ask for healing of the church. I don't ask God to reveal to me where I am needed and then get involved. I don't ask Jesus to come into the weak part of my personality and strengthen it to do His work. What might I be missing, I must ask myself.

I surely prayed for Gene, though. I prayed that God would show me where I was needed and help me understand what we needed to do to help Gene remain as healthy as he could be. I prayed that I would know how to move our lives forward with improved health. I asked for strength where we were weak and wisdom to improve what we were already doing. I was open to ways I could be involved and helpful in his care.

Trusting our source

We felt financially weak. Gene had Medicare and supplemental insurance, but if I didn't work, how would we meet our daily needs? Gene was still able to do some accounting and kept as many of his clients as possible. Since work was his life, it did keep him distracted from worry or speculations. Working also caused him stress—his eyes were not as good as they needed to be, and he tired easily.

He needed me to drive him to pick up and deliver his clients' papers and to do some of the computer work. He also needed me to help him with his dialysis and to drive him to his doctor and nurse clinics. I didn't see how I could hold down a job and be a partner to him.

I wanted to go to his clinics with him so I could hear what the doctor or nurse said to him firsthand. I also wanted to be sure they got the whole story and not just, "Everything is okay." I had promised that I would go through this with him, and I didn't want to be preoccupied with a job and all the tasks that need to be done around the house on a daily basis. Being with Gene and helping him through this seemed like a top priority, but how would we make it?

"You, Father, are the source of everything. You are able to supply our needs through any source You want because You are the true source of everything. You can provide through Gene's accounting, through our home-based business, or some other way that we have not thought about," I prayed.

We had the health product business that Gene and I were involved in, but that was only paying for our product use. I didn't know what would happen, but I was sure God would come through for us. Gene's setback had taken the wind out of my sails. Some people with acute kidney disease can get their function back, but Gene's health problems were not limited to kidney failure. Kidney failure just complicated Gene's health challenges.

A couple of days later, our neighbor stopped by to tell us that he was going to get some irrigation equipment for his fields and that the planned location of the system would probably cause water to shoot onto the empty field of our property. He asked if that was a problem.

Since I had already started thinking a little bit about what I would do when Gene passed on, I told him that Gene was not doing well and that he could possibly die in the next few years. I told him that after Gene's death, I would probably sell the house and move near my brother. So I didn't really care what happened in our empty field.

A week later we got a call from our neighbor's parents, who owned the farm he was farming. Our field jutted out into the middle of their fields, and with our permission, they had been grazing their cows there for the last few years. They also used it as a shortcut to their barn. They wanted to come over and talk to us about an idea they had.

Their idea was to buy our field. Since the separate sale of the field would lower the amount I could get for the house, they wanted to buy the house too, giving us a lifetime lease. We wouldn't pay rent, only property taxes and insurance.

It was an amazing deal, and we had quite a bit of equity in the house. The equity would help us with living expenses in a wonderful, blessed way. We took the offer and vowed to live frugally. We had never imagined such a plan, but God had surely provided. This was another of the many ways we would see God intimately involved in our lives.

Waning but not worthless

Although Gene had his accounting, he was feeling that his purpose for living was gone. One of the men in our Sunday school class thought it would be a good idea to start having a monthly community dinner in our fellowship hall. We would take turns planning the meal and preparing it so that no one would get burnt out on the idea. If we were blessed to find twelve people to take the lead, any member of the class would only have to be in charge once a year.

Gene was very excited about the idea, and his entrepreneurial personality took off with ideas about how to reach out to the community and help the attendance grow. We volunteered for the second month. Another important aspect of Gene's mental health needs was covered. He was given peace of mind over our finances. He could rely on me to be there when he needed me. Now he also had a purpose.

Gene put a lot of thought into the menu for our dinner and where we could shop to keep the expenses down. He had an idea to have a drawing for a free dinner for two each month. In filling out their ticket, the participants would provide information to contact them if they won and information to send out flyers to advertise the next dinner. He also had plans for entertainment, which none of the class liked, but still he was planning and feeling vital. Churches have many needs, and God will bring ministries to those who pray.

I was not quite as excited about the dinners as he was. I thought it was a good idea and was glad to see Gene have that old spark of excitement back. I was worried that he would overdo and that I would have to do most of the work while also worrying about him becoming weak and falling. We were able to recruit a team of helpers, and it was a fun night. We served nearly a hundred people, and we had a true feeling of accomplishment as we left the church that night. Everything in the kitchen and fellowship hall had been cleaned up. The next morning Gene was planning ways to make his drawing for meals more effective.

Goals with God 101

This could almost sound like a "pray and the magic begins" chapter, but that is not what happened. Praying and journaling help us set goals, and it does not matter whether we actually think of it as goal setting or not. We secure the thoughts in our minds so that we are more open to the opportunities God brings into our lives. For instance, the thought that Gene might only have three more years to live started me thinking about what I would do on my own.

As much as I didn't want to think about those possibilities, I knew it was best for me to have a few plans even if they changed a hundred times in the meantime. If I had not had thoughts about Gene's passing, I would not have mentioned to our neighbor that I would be selling the house, and he would not have talked to his parents. More importantly, if I had not asked God to go before me in this whole journey of caregiving, I might not have been open to His leadership.

As it is stated in Ephesians 3:20 (NIV), "Now to him who is able to do immeasurably more than all we ask or imagine according to his power at work in us."

Gifts from God

We can grip what is visible so tightly that we miss the extravagant gifts God wants to give us. John W. Peterson wrote, "He owns the cattle on a thousand hills, the wealth in every mine … … he is my Father, so they're mine as well," in his hymn based on Psalm 50. It's not that God withholds benefits like a miserly grandfather who only has his paltry savings or earthly wealth to draw from.

God is the source of everything we need. We may not be able to understand fully God's extravagant love for us or his desire to help us. We can trust God. Trusting God means we can believe we will get an answer to our prayers if we are willing to keep our eyes and heart open to the possibilities around us.

Answers to prayers don't necessarily happen all at once; sometimes the answer comes in bits or pieces that will fit together when the time is right. Sometimes one obedient, seemingly unrelated step can put a whole process in motion. I don't really know how to explain this effect, and maybe if I could, I would be as wise as God … and, well, I'm not.

I don't understand how my TV can pick up waves from the air so that when I turn it on and tune it to a certain channel, there is the program I want to watch in color and with sound. The fact that I don't understand how the picture appears does not keep me from trusting my TV or that I will get the station I want every time. Likewise, we may not understand how God works on our behalf when we need Him, but that should not keep us from trusting Him.

In 1 Peter 5:6–7, the Apostle Peter wrote, "Humble yourselves, (be obedient, trusting God more than yourself) therefore, under God's mighty hand, that he may lift you up in due time (when God knows you really need it). Cast all your anxieties on him, for he cares for you." I added a little specificity in parentheses.

Trust and obey.

Here is an illustration from my life. No magical or special effects are involved—only an odd series of events. Something within me, told me to start knitting a simple children's sweater pattern and to make many of them. I believe God provided that motivation. The nagging impulse wouldn't go away, no matter how stupid I thought it was. Somehow I had the idea that if I was obedient, Gene and I would be taken care of financially.

Those were totally unrelated ideas—making children's sweaters would result in no financial stress. I obediently started making the sweaters. I got serious about making them after a few years of reluctance. When the time was right, I took the idea seriously, and I have not had anxiety over money again. This is a true story! I believe God called me to make the sweaters. I didn't know why, but eventually I trusted the impulse I had to make the sweaters. I trusted God's calling and that he cares about my needs. (Matthew 6: 25-33) I also trusted Him as my ultimate source of care. As I said before I do not understand God's ways, but that does not keep me from trusting him. I can only say that our situation seemed much bigger than we were….a mountain size bigger. I cast all my cares upon Him because it was all I knew to do. God may have something totally different for you. Is God asking you to be obedient in something? Humble yourself, no matter how crazy it seems, and see how God blesses you. Acknowledging his gift and praising him for it is our act of worship. I don't want you to think there is magic in the process. Seeking God is the most important act anyone can do. Too often we seek the blessing of God and never really seek to know God. It is never about the blessing; it is always about His presence. God doesn't bless us because we are good or even because we deserve a blessing. He blesses us when we seek him and desire Him, as it is written in Matthew 6:33.

Pray first. Then keep your eyes open to his prompting. Take a step in obedience to what you may hear God saying to you. As the Apostle Peter wrote in 1 Peter 5:7, "Cast all your cares upon Him, for He cares for you."

CHAPTER 5

Find Time Alone with God

Yet the Lord longs to be gracious to you; therefore he will rise up to show you compassion.

--Isaiah 30:18

"God is our refuge and our strength, an ever-present help in trouble."

--Psalm 46:1

"I can do everything through him who gives me strength."

--Philippians 4:13

Burnout prevention

Caregivers must be careful about burnout. A loved one who is ill can be cranky. The caregiver often takes the brunt of the loved one's bad mood. One of my friends told me, early in Gene's dialysis phase, that I needed to look at Gene clinically. If I did not step back from the situation emotionally, I would take his moods too personally. Looking at his situation clinically would put distance between the situation and my emotions. I needed to be able to distance myself from his emotions so I could stay rational and composed through his care.

I was glad to be home with Gene and be able to help him, but I also needed an outlet or time away from him for just myself. Even with scheduled time away, I would forget and become involved in his emotions.

This is funny now, and it was a little funny then. Each morning I would ask Gene how his night had gone and how he felt. As his health became worse, his complaints became numerous. Each morning I would expect the common answer we expect when we ask such questions: "Oh, I'm fine." I don't know why. As his heath declined, however, his complaints intensified. After some months of this routine, I told him that I started every morning depressed because all he ever did was complain about how he felt. I'm not sure how I expected him to answer me. He told me that if I didn't want to know how he felt, then I should stop asking. Of course! What was I thinking? It made me laugh.

Getting emotional and mental strength

Our church happened to be a Stephen Ministries church. Stephen Ministers are members of the church who go through a fifty-hour training program to learn how to help other members of the congregation through all sorts of difficult life situations. Stephen Ministers will supply a listening ear and moral support for anyone experiencing any problem—losing a job, raising a troubled teen, or caring for someone with a terminal illness. These are situations that need a listening ear and someone to review concerns or solutions.

Our pastor suggested that I might want to have a Stephen Minister help me through the years ahead. I talked to the head of the program and was assigned a Stephen Minister. My Stephen Minister happened to be the nurse who had come to Gene's aid in church when he had leaned his head on the pew ahead of him. We met once a week at a local coffee café for an hour. The focus was me and my problems or successes. She listened and encouraged me. That hour per week that was all about me was an anchor in my life. Acknowledging my loss of dreams and abilities by talking about it to a neutral person worked wonders in helping me move on from a state of loss to a state of fresh ideas and new directions.

There are so many losses in caring for a loved one who is ill. The caregiver faces the loss of a carefree shared lifestyle, free time, control over one's schedule, dreams … the list goes on. The biggest, I think, is the loss of dreams you and your loved one had together. These losses are real, and their emotional pain could go unnoticed or ignored because of the urgency of caregiving. Never forget, however, that you are important too! Dreams change sometimes, but they can still go on.

Friends, of course, would have met with me to listen and offer advice. After a point, however, I would have either felt like a burden to them or actually become one. With my Stephen Minister, I could let it all out if I wanted and know that what I said was going no further. The café was a wonderful place to meet, partly because it was not very busy and allowed us the privacy we needed and partly because they made an awesome café mocha.

Because the café was quiet, it also was a good place for me to read, journal, or just be. I needed time alone to sort out my feelings and just have time for myself.

Once Gene was dressed and settled at his desk, he was fine. I had a cell phone, and the cafe was only a five-minute drive away. The owner was very congenial and compassionate. He spoiled me when he knew my situation, allowing me special privileges—a cup of coffee as a refill after a chai tea, whipped cream on my plain coffee, solitude when I needed it, or friendship when I needed that. It was a total time of refreshment, which gave me a much better attitude. Through this café and its owner, I truly felt, God was providing what I needed. I didn't have to feel selfish because my private time there did make me easier to be around, and sometimes Gene liked having the house to himself. Stress and anxiety do not do us any favors. As I look back on this period and the fact that I live in a small resort town, I can see how blessed I was to have such a great place to go and to be a member of a church that had a Stephen Ministry. These are benefits that I believe God had put in place. Of course many others benefited from them, but if you knew our small town and the little it has to offer … having these simple enjoyments were rich treasures for my soul. Some churches have a coffee ministry in their buildings during the week and others have trained Christian counselors. There are probably many ministries offered by churches or organizations to offer respite and encouragement to the hurting and overwhelmed.

That is what I did for my peace, but there are other ways of relieving stress. If you like to exercise or watch the morning news while sipping coffee, or a quiet time of prayer or Bible study, do that. Keep a routine to provide an anchor in your day. Start your day as normally as possible. You may have a new standard for what is normal for most of your life, but keep some part of your "old normal" just for you.

God is gracious, as the Bible tells us, and I love this comment in Isaiah 30:18: "He rises to show you compassion." We are our own worst judge. We never have mercy on ourselves; if we do, we feel guilty. Eventually we feel we must do task after task. We get the idea that if we don't do all these tasks, the world will fall apart. I can imagine God at this point, rising from his throne to show us compassion. "I've got this situation" He might say. "Take a rest. It's okay. You can take a breath and relax a little."

Your health is important.

When we are anxious or afraid, our breathing can become shallow, and our lungs do not fully inflate. I am sure you know that the body needs oxygen to clean our blood and stimulate our cells. Gene had muscle aches mostly at night. His chiropractor told him to breathe more deeply. He was to take ten deep breaths and relax. When Gene did that, he did get quick relief from muscle aches.

As caregivers, we need our muscles to be strong and healthy for support and lifting. Those muscles can get tired and ache from the stress on them. I heard someone suggest that in the morning, when waking, we should consciously breathe deeply from the diaphragm for ten minutes while sitting on the side of the bed. As you become accustomed to doing this, you can add some stretches at the same time. This will refresh your body and prepare it for the day ahead.

If you feel overwhelmed or anxious at any time during the day, try deep, slow breaths in through the nose and out through the mouth. You could add meditation to your breathing exercise by thinking,

"God is" as you take a deep breath and "my help" as you slowly let the air out and relax.

Be sure to get fresh air and sunshine when you can. If your loved one is having a bad day and you are getting the brunt of it, take a short walk or sit near a window and breathe once the situation is settled.

Warnings about too much sun have influenced us so much that we have almost forgotten that sunshine is good for us. The sun is known to boost the body's vitamin D supply. At least a thousand different genes governing virtually every tissue in the body are now thought to be regulated by the active form of vitamin D. Vitamin D is synthesized through the skin more readily than when obtained through food. Medical professionals recommend ten minutes of sunshine every day for adequate absorption of vitamin D.

Other body hormones such as serotonin, melatonin, and other endorphins are dependent on sunlight, fresh air, and darkness at appropriate times. Sunshine and darkness and fresh air are free, God-given blessings you can utilize.

Fresh water seems to be more of a luxury these days than in days gone by. Today we buy bottled water and water filtration systems to be sure our water is healthy. Water plays an important role in regulating body temperature, transporting nutrients and oxygen to cells, cushioning joints, and protecting organs and tissues.

The body has many ways to signal its need for water: joint pain, depression, fatigue, headache, or heartburn. Some of the best water to drink is filtered water, spring water, or reverse osmosis water. How much water should you drink? A simple formula is to take your weight and divide it by two. That is how many ounces of water you should drink for your health. I'm not a big fan of water and find it hard to drink that much water per day; I find that I do not require a lot of liquid to feel happy. A dietician told me that my feelings are not what I should go by, and that by the time I feel thirsty, I am probably already close to mild dehydration. She suggested carrying a bottle of water with me wherever I go and taking sips of it all through my day.

I also do not like the blandness of water. For that reason, I boil some berries in a medium pot of water. I drink it hot or cold. It has no added, processed sugar and gives me a little flavor in my water. If you have a weak bladder, do not drink after 6:00 PM for less interruption of your night's sleep.

Know your limits.

I found that I could handle the regular flow of events. However, when some other unrelated responsibility was added to my schedule, I would become physically ill and have to go to bed. Sometimes going to bed is possible, and sometimes it is not.

Although I was talking to a Stephen Minister, I think I was not being totally honest with her. I think I was keeping a lot of feelings pent up. I don't think I ever got to the bottom of my fears about caring for Gene or what would happen when the end was here. Wanting to look like a pillar of strength, I was tearing myself up inside. My pride was ruining my health. Any sort of extra activity would make me physically ill.

I remember that I never wanted to let a conversation turn to sympathetic feelings toward me—not just with my Stephen Minister, but at any time. I never wanted to feel any weakness or look honestly at the situation. I thought if I thought I was strong and never admitted weakness or need, I would stay strong. I brushed off any words of sympathy or concern. I was making myself sick by suppressing my true feelings and not willingly looking at them.

I felt that my life was like a house of cards; it was so delicately balanced that if even one event or breath of air touched it slightly, the whole structure would fall down. I didn't have the strength to rebuild it. Life had started coming at us at alarming speed, and I didn't want anything to wreck what I had started. I just didn't have the strength to start over. As I started working in the home healthcare industry, I found other caregivers feeling the same way. They were always saying that they could handle their situations. Then one day they would be saying they were not sure life was worth living. One caregiver caused such concern that I took her to our pastor to pray. We need to be honest about our fears and the stress that caregiving can cause and seek help.

Don't neglect to go the doctor yourself. Caregiving is more than a full-time job. It can seem that we have no time for ourselves, but we need to take care of ourselves too. Be sure to schedule regular checkups with your doctor for yourself. You are important, and you need care too. Caregivers often feel guilty caring for themselves or spoiling themselves. You are worth that effort, though, and it is important. I will say it again: You are worth a little spoiling.

When people are ill, their world becomes all about them. Schedules are arranged around doctor appointments, treatments, therapy, help to get to the bathroom, meals, and social interaction. It is easy for them to lose sight of the bigger picture and the fact that their caregivers have lives of their own. Caregivers should sit with them and discuss both persons' needs and the caregivers' need for time to themselves or with friends—not necessarily long periods of time, just some time. Most people can understand that need.

If they are unsettled about being alone, find a friend of the family or a family member to stay for a little while so that you may go out for dinner or even a movie with a friend. Caregiving and receiving care needs to be a mutual agreement. At intervals, sit and talk about what is going on for both of you.

We were fortunate and had a good group of friends (I believe that our helpful friends were also provided by God. You will see how great they were before this book is over.) The men organized a card game once a week, and that allowed me to have the house to myself, which seemed a luxury. When Gene was too weak to go to the games, they came to our house. I was glad to host the games and provide coffee and snacks to have an hour or two to myself. On Tuesday evenings we attended a Bible study at some friend's home. They were good about helping me with Gene at the time, and the interaction with mutual friends was great ... not to mention the spiritual growth achieved together.

If you feel the need to spend a weekend or week with friends, check with home healthcare services in your area. These agencies have trained people who can stay with your loved one. This extended getaway time is important for your mental, emotional, and physical health. Do not feel guilty; just prepare by having dependable help in place.

In my area, we have a "care home" center for some social events and a few rooms for those in need of caregiving to come and spend a few days. The staff is trained, and some such facilities may have a nurse on call. Check your local yellow pages to see if such a home may be in your area. A friend of mine used to schedule a massage once a week to spoil herself while she was caring for her husband with end-stage cancer. Think about what would give you solace in the midst of your journey. Feeling drained will only cause more problems.

Keeping your head above water

I heard a story about a swimmer who took a dive into a lake and started swimming. As he was swimming, a dense fog came over the lake. The swimmer started to panic because he could not see the shore. He would swim one way, panic, and change direction. His heart raced faster and faster as he became more and more confused, swimming in one direction and then another in hope of finding the shore. His breathing became more labored. To conserve his energy, he turned on his back to float and rest. As he calmed down, he could hear voices coming from the shore. He started to swim again toward the voices.

This story, I think, is a good illustration of what can happen in the middle of constant caregiving. We start to feel overwhelmed and get confused about the best tactics, especially as medical situations or emergencies start happening at an inordinate rate. Sometimes it is essential for the caregiver to take a break, a rest to conserve energy and creativity. A rest can help you hear God's directions or your own intuition and keep you cheerful. It is not a weakness to need a vacation; a vacation is a necessity.

A problem may arise if you do take time away. I know it was a problem for me and others. Your loved one has become so dependent on you that taking time away seems very selfish. Dependence makes your loved one afraid while you are away. If you have found good help or a safe place for your loved one to stay, do not take that insecurity personally. I remember when my husband told me I was the most selfish person he knew, although I had been with him through all his treatments and was spending the whole day at the hospital with him. When necessary, I had spent many other days there, and nights as well. Not to mention how my life ... well, you get the picture. I was angry, and I told him so. My anger did not help, and I didn't feel any better after letting off that steam. In such situations we need to look at the situation clinically, as my friend suggested, and go for a walk. Do not accept the guilt.

Social media can be a good way to stay in touch with others, ask for prayer, read a few funny jokes, and stay aware of the world. Sometimes there are even support groups you can join on a national level through social media, or you can join a local support group that meets in your area. Through Wordpress.com, you can start a blog for free, and you can be totally honest there. Mostly no one will see it unless you advertise it. No one understands what you are going through like the others who are going through the same experience too. Join the discussion at my blog: Caregivingboost.com. There is no need to feel alone. Many people in this country are going through the same struggle. They may need to hear from you, and they can encourage you too.

One step at a time

Eating a healthy diet is always important anytime, but with the added stress of caregiving, it is very important. Make sure you are eating enough whole foods, not just quick processed foods. It has been proven that those foods with the brightest colors are the best for us because they have the most nutrition, so make a colorful plate of food. Caffeine seems like a good pick-me-up, but too much can let us down hard in the long run. Energy drinks are not the answer. Eating whole foods in a rainbow of colors and drinking filtered water are two of best dietary practices to help yourself feel better and stronger.

The average American consumes five pounds of food in a day. Over your lifetime, that's about seventy tons of food that will pass through your intestinal tract and be assimilated by your body. It does matter what you eat. If you don't like to cook or plan new menus or you feel that you are too old to change, I understand. Even though I was willing to try new ways of eating, my husband wasn't, and I didn't want to add more stress for either him or me. The old adages are true. Rome wasn't built in a day, and a thousand-mile journey starts with one step. So take a step or two in the right direction and eventually add more new steps toward healthy eating. The foods that are causing disease and killing Americans are foods that are overly processed and high in sugar and man-made fats and oils.

A simple first step may be adding a salad or freshly cut vegetables or fruit to your meals. Try a bread with more fiber than white bread and work up to whole grain. Lean meats, poultry, and baked or grilled fish are good choices. A nurse practitioner told my husband to think *fins and feathers* when choosing meats because poultry and fish are easiest to digest. Any healthy choice is better than no steps at all toward a healthier diet. Slowly your body will start to crave healthier foods.

Of course there are still dietary factors you will need to watch. Gene had started on a blood thinner when he developed some heart problems. It was spring, and we had leaf lettuce in the garden. For lunch and dinner, I would fix nice salads with lettuce, cucumbers, and other veggies. The lab wanted Gene to come in on a regular basis for testing until they could determine the ideal level of blood thinner for him to take. They were having a horrible time, and it seemed his blood was getting thinner than it should be at the level of blood thinner he was taking. The nurse asked me if we were eating lettuce and/or cucumbers with any frequency. When I told her about our wonderful, healthy fresh lettuce salads with cucumbers at lunch and dinner, she told me to stop. Lettuce and cucumbers apparently have an effect on our blood. Talk to your health professionals about dietary changes. There is never too much communication.

The atmosphere at any meal should be joyful. Keep the conversation pleasant. Turn off the TV. Don't use meals to bring up troubling topics. Think about the good times and the victories in your day. Stress has poor effects on digestion.

Nurturing your soul

It is important for us to understand that our outward attitudes and behavior are almost always products of our inner spirit. We are multifaceted. We are not just physical beings; we have a spiritual side as well. In Matthew 12:34b, Jesus says, "For the mouth speaks what the heart is full of." Keeping our feelings pent up is likely to cause us to blow up at inappropriate times or when we feel pressured by the day's activities.

Someone once said the best psychiatrist's couch is the Holy Spirit. By spending time reading a poetic book of the Bible, such as the Psalms, each day and pouring out our hearts in prayer, we give ourselves great therapy sessions. Don't worry that God cannot handle your anger, your fears, your fatigue. God wants us to cast our cares on Him. Prayer has been shown in many studies to be helpful, and articles have been written on the benefits of prayer.

I found that I could calm myself and strengthen my soul through a Bible study that I could do on my own at home and meditate on the truths I found during my study. There are many good studies on the market. Some are on books of the Bible, and some are on topics that may interest you. A good and helpful independent study method is reading a psalm a day and finding the words that describe an action or attribute of God.

Psalm 1
Blessed is the man
Who does not walk in the counsel
Of the wicked
Or stand in the way of sinners,
Or sit in the seat of mockers.
But his delight is in the law of the
Lord
And on his law he meditates day
And night.
He is like a tree planted by streams
Of water
Which yields its fruit in season
And whose leaf does not wither
Whatever he does prospers.

Not so with the wicked!
They are like chaff
That the wind blows away
Therefore the wicked will not stand
In the judgment seat
Nor sinners in the assembly of the
Righteous.

For the Lord watches over the way
Of the Righteous,
But the way of the wicked will
Perish.

In careful, meditative reading of this psalm, we can see immediately that the Lord watches over the righteous (us). By inference, we see that God gives prosperity to those who meditate on His law (read and learn from God's Word). I would take an index card, write "intimate" at the top, and then write Psalm 1. God is watching over me, and He makes me prosper me when I honor His Word. In an alphabetized file box, I would file that card under *I* for *intimate*. I would then spend a little time thinking about how I saw God as an intimate in my life and praise Him for those times I saw Him as my intimate.

I would make a separate card for "Prospers." Put Psalm 1:3 on that card and file it. Spend time thinking about when I felt God had helped me with finances in some way or I felt that my spiritual understanding had prospered. Spend time praising God for it. By doing this for yourself you can create a file of spiritual strength for yourself.

The next day I would read Psalm 2 and look for phrases or words reflecting activities or attributes of God. This activity is not a test. If you don't see one, it is okay. You can pray that God will reveal to you what He wants you to see. Remember—just the day before, we found that God is intimate, and we understand that to mean that He is involved with us, so He will help us.

As the days go on, you may have times when you need to remember that God is intimate and involved with you, and you can go to your file and find the card. As you continue on in this study of God's attributes, you may find a psalm that also says that God is intimate or makes us prosperous. Take the appropriate card out and write the new scriptural reference on the card. Now you have two Scriptures of reference when you need to remember that God is intimate with us and helps us prosper. When you have finished doing this with all of the hundred and fifty psalms, you will have trained yourself to see God's attributes in almost all Scriptures and have a ready file of attributes to use as you need them. What a blessing!

Excerpts from *Eat This and Live*, Don Colbert, MD, Copyright 2009, published by Siloam, a Strang Company.

CHAPTER 6

Use All Your Resources

He who dwells in the shelter of the Most High will rest in the shadow of the Almighty.

--Psalm 91:1

Come to Me, all you who are weary and burdened, and I will give you rest.

--Matthew 11:28

Teamwork

The nephrologists and CAPD nurses on Gene's medical team were so helpful. Our dialysis supplies came from a very reliable source. They would call once a month, and I would tell them what supplies I had on hand. They would be in touch with the nurses and learn what Gene's condition was, how he was doing, and what direction the nurses wanted to go with his therapy. A week later, the appropriate supplies would be delivered to our door and stacked where I wanted them.

The delivery man was very thoughtful, and we had fun speaking with him. He and Gene would have quite a talk about "man stuff" and other topics. Gene looked forward to the deliveries. If I had any questions at any time, I could call the CAPD nurses, and they were very patient and caring.

Once a month we would have a nurse's clinic at the dialysis center. Every other month we had a doctor's clinic as well. We had plenty of support. However, there were many factors to watch for on a regular basis. If you are facing dialysis, you will find this guidance helpful. If dialysis is not a part of your care plan, please bear with me. You will find your own support team with your doctors and nurses.

For dialysis patients

Initially, Gene did four exchanges a day and none during the night. We later changed to a machine called a cycler. The cycler did four exchanges through the night. Then Gene did one manual exchange at midday. We needed to monitor his blood pressure each time to know the strength of solution to use. We needed to watch his fluid and sugar intake. One might think watching the sugar intake would be pretty routine for a diabetic, but Gene loved sugar as most diabetics do, and he was not careful. Peritoneal dialysis fluid is a mixture of dextrose, which is a sugar, salt, and other minerals. Sugar levels may be hard to control. These are issues that you will want to talk about at the scheduled clinics if your loved one is diabetic or on dialysis.

Factors to consider

We live in northern Indiana. Our winters can be very cold and sometimes icy, windy, and snowy, causing snowdrifts. It is a good idea to call your power company and let them know your situation so they are aware that you have a supply of dialysis fluid that must have temperatures above freezing and below 100°F. You will want to make sure the utility company knows that someone in your household is very ill and that in the case of a power outage, you should have first priority for assistance.

We had a power outage once, and I called the dialysis fluid company for information on what to do. They said to move the fluid away from outside wall, cover it with blankets, and call the power company to let them know my situation. Peritoneal dialysis can be done manually, but some patients use the electric cycler, which does exchanges through the night. The cycler is electrically powered, which is another reason to let your power company know your situation. All these details can be talked over with your doctors or nurses and should not make you worry.

Make any outage situation easy on yourself by contacting the utility company, the highway department, or any other office that may be able to help you with your situation in a time of emergency. Other home healthcare scenarios may involve oxygen machines, lifts, or other important equipment that runs on electricity. If there is a power outage or an early morning doctor appointment or emergency and you have already informed the proper organizations, they will be quick to help you.

We happen to live in a small rural community. I'm sure that our location helped us. One time the electricity went out at our house, and it was nearly time for Gene to start on his dialysis cycler at night.

We were amazed that there was no power in the whole house except the wall with the outlet where the cycler was plugged in. We started Gene on his treatment, and I called the utility company. They were here in short order and found that ice had condensed on one of the wires in the transformer and had caused the partial outage. It was quickly repaired. The fact that the only outlet that had electricity was the one where the cycler was plugged in seemed like a miracle to us. God works in mysterious ways, as the saying goes.

Talk to your spouse's hairstylist to see if he or she will come to your house. We always like to feel that we are looking as good as we can, and sometimes a haircut can make a big difference in attitude.

Gene was very resistant to doctors and very suspicious of their motives. I was blessed to have one of Gene's sons nearby. I could call him to help me convince Gene when he needed to go to the hospital and to go by ambulance when that was important. Sometimes Gene would just refuse to go the hospital or even take his medications. Sometimes his friends would encourage him to take care of himself too. I think Gene was particularly stubborn about this, but the same can be true of anyone. Do you know whom you can call if you need help convincing your loved one? Sometimes it would only take a phone call to his son; sometimes Greg had to come to us.

Teaming with your loved one

One great resource you have is your loved one. It is good that in these days, women are partnering more with their husbands to get household chores done. The old, stereotypical division of household labor is mostly a relic of the past. If you haven't started paying the bills, the period while your loved one is still feeling well would be a good time to get involved. The same goes for knowing where the lockbox keys are, where the key to the lawnmower is, how to start and use the snow blower, where the household's favorite groceries are bought, where the fuse box is and which switch goes to what area. Talk with your loved one about the household activities he or she handled and learn how to manage these tasks.

My friend was so glad that her husband had showed her how to use the tractor and snow plow before he could no longer operate them. My dad had to take a hinge off the lock box to get it open after my mom died because he didn't know where she kept the keys. Know where all the important papers are. No one wants to think about the inevitable. Sadly, however, it is still the inevitable. Sit down, have some coffee, and talk about these matters; get out and do those tasks that are still new to you.

Sit with your loved one and talk about medical procedures he or she wants done or omitted in any medical crises during which the sick person cannot speak. Most doctors' offices will give you a form called a "living will." They will urge this document upon you as your loved one becomes more ill.

Living wills are good, though we avoided this issue because we just didn't want to think about it. There are forms on the Internet that give you an idea of how to make one if your doctor doesn't give you one. A website you can go to is www.caringinfo.org. Click on "living wills."

You may decide that you don't want life support ... meaning being kept alive by machine. However, there are levels of life support that you may not have considered. Gene slipped into a coma unexpectedly at the hospital. As they were carting him to the ICU, they asked me if they should insert a feeding tube. Technically, a feeding tube is a form of life support—but so is dialysis. I didn't know what to do. Gene was in the hospital that time because an aneurism had burst. It burst onto his brain stem, which made him unable to swallow well, and he had lost his appetite.

His neurologist had suggested that if Gene did not show any sign of desire for food, I should just "let Gene go." Gene had not shown a desire to eat; now he was in a coma, and I had a split second to decide what to do. Neither option (letting him go or inserting a feeding tube) sounded promising, nor had we talked about feeding tubes. Of course I wanted to honor his feelings; even more, I wanted him to live, so I consented to the feeding tube. He recovered from the coma and resented the feeding tube, which was attached to his nose and extended down his throat and into his stomach. It was not saving his life, only prolonging his suffering. Because his dialysis port was in his abdomen and he was using his peritoneal lining to do his dialysis, they could not insert a stomach tube.

Knowing what he wanted would have saved us that pain. The doctors and nurses will read the living will and will honor it. They will act according to the will so that you can be supportive to your loved one in any circumstance. You will question your decisions in many situations, but if you and your loved one have discussed the most important treatment issues and agreed on them, you can make the best decision even in a split second.

We are not God.

When someone is with another person 24/7, especially a spouse or child, something happens. This change is not beneficial to anyone. I saw it in myself, and I have seen it in the family members of clients I have cared for as a home healthcare aid. I can imagine it is the number one cause of burnout and family conflict. It happens without us being aware. Gail Sheehy makes a good point in her book, "Passages in

Caregiving". After we have been caregivers for a while we start to feel quite confident. Our loved one and we have established a routine. We can sense what our loved one wants before they ask. We make it look easy. Our friends think we are a hero caring for our loved one and we start to think so too. Ms. Sheehy points out that we are Playing God.

I often thought I was in control of our situation, but I truly had control over very little. I certainly did not have control over his disease, his acceptance of it or his need to follow instructions. I couldn't control his comfort much of the time or his moods. The only thing I could control were my moods, attitude and my actions.

No one wants to be a pessimist, nor do we want to give up hope, but we can only do so much. Then we must trust the professionals and allow God to work through them. Prayer is our greatest resource, especially when we feel totally helpless. Again, do not hesitate to pour your heart out to God. We are not God, but we have an amazing God who cares.

For me, codependency was a real downfall. I enjoyed feeling needed and having a purpose. Certainly it was tiring and restrictive, but it felt good too. Gene and I had grown closer and talked about matters that we should have been talking about over the years. We had become best friends, and our troubled marriage seemed part of the past. For the first time in our marriage, I was in charge, and it felt good. I was making this whole caregiving situation work. Gene's six children were looking to me for his care. I was needed, by golly, and it felt good. Each morning I woke with a purpose. Even when we are really not in control, we like to feel that we are in control. We like to believe we have all the details covered.

With the Internet and iPhones, we can be in touch with each other all the time. I would send out emails telling the children how Gene was doing. Every other night, while he was in the hospital or rehab, I would email them an update of hope. Even when some doctors gave us no hope, I still believed we could beat his situation. The problem was that some of the doctors did give us a window of hope if Gene was willing to fight. He always said he wanted to fight and was able to do so, but in truth he wasn't. I wasn't able to help him, either. We grabbed onto hope for dear life, but it was a façade.

The facts were the facts. Short of an extreme miracle, nothing was going to change. So my emails were not quite true. I didn't lie; I just didn't face the truth. That, in turn, caused false hope within the other family members. No one has to be brutally honest, but the truth is still the best policy. The truth is best even if the truth is, "I don't know what to think or what is going on." Playing God makes people think they have to have the answer, and sometimes there is no answer.

I rose early every morning to go to the hospital an hour away. I stayed all day until Gene had tried to eat some dinner and was settled for the evening. I told myself that anything at home could wait. What if the doctor came and I wasn't there? Who would explain everything? "Gene needs me," I told myself. We talk to ourselves a lot about how important we think we are.

Finally my Stephen Minister told me, after I had a meltdown, that I needed to take at least one day off a week just to be. I should talk with friends, go to the library, or get tasks done at the house in a relaxed manner. I did as advised, and I found that having a day that was just a normal day—no watching Gene suffer, no doctors or nurses, no stuffy rooms—was so healing for me. My day off gave me a new perspective on my life as a caregiver.

I notified the family that I wanted to take one day a week off and asked if they would be sure to visit Gene on that day. That way I knew Gene was cared for by the doctors and nurses and getting visits from his kids or his sister at least once a week. I could relax and know I had one day to do whatever I wanted or needed to do without added guilt. If there isn't a family member nearby, maybe a group of friends would schedule their visits to give you your day off.

Seeking help

I am offering this advice in the assumption that you do not have a full-time, demanding job. If you do have a forty-hour job outside your home *and* you are spending your evenings and weekends at the hospital or in constant care at home, that workload is too much. Even well-intentioned humans are breakable. Don't be ashamed to admit you have needs. Consider contacting a home healthcare agency to arrange for someone to come into your home. Many times a home healthcare worker will come in for a few hours and give you a break, not only from caregiving, but also from regular daily housekeeping chores. They will spend time comforting your loved one with foot massages, a friendly smile, new conversations about life outside the four walls, and new jokes or stories. They can help you by doing light housecleaning and laundry. The home healthcare company will help you explore ways to finance the help and make a schedule.

Breaking the monotony

There are ways to break the monotony of day-to-day activities. After Gene's eyesight became so poor that he couldn't even read large print, we began reading books together and discussing them. It was great stimulation for Gene, and it was something we could do together that was fun. The problem was that Gene typically had been napping on and off all day while I had been carrying the workload around the house. Gene wanted to read until the wee hours of the morning, and by then I was hoarse and tired. There would have been nothing wrong with stopping earlier in the evening. Only my guilt prevented a timely stop. There is no need for guilt. Remember that we are humans, not gods.

There are games and puzzles that can be done together. Crosswords are always good to do as a team. A fun game Gene and I use to play was trying to remember old TV shows. Granted, it sounds a little boring, but it turned out to be funny and pleasurable.

Another fun pastime is going through pictures and remembering the ages of the children in the pictures or who that long-forgotten relative is. You and your loved one might even work on a scrapbook. Invite the grandchildren in on the project and talk about relatives they may have forgotten or have never known.

Sometimes we or our loved one might start playing the "if only" game. Generally this game makes us feel worse about our situation. Instead of a negative game, make it a fun game. What if our noses kept growing? What if we were totally bionic? What if I had an arm coming out of my back? Why not be silly and laugh instead of crying?

Blessed be the family

Then there are the family members who live far away but insist that they know more than you do about your loved one's care. They call to give you instructions on how to do the tasks you are already doing. Being tired or feeling overwhelmed can make the simplest word of advice seem like judgment. It can seem that they are suggesting that you are not doing a good enough job. Listen politely, be courteous, and when the call is over, take some deep breaths or do some stretches or get out that journal. It is okay to give what they say some thought and politely let it go if it doesn't really apply or make your situation easier or better.

Most family members want to help but may not be able to be involved. They are thinking of you when they hear or read something they think could be helpful. Such information might be material that you need to know. I know that when Gene's three sons were trying to be helpful, their efforts came across as criticism, and I reacted from that attitude. I remembered times past when they were not so supportive of me, and it felt like they were against me because those old feelings popped up. When there is no filter because we are tired, it is not a good time to react. We were all worried and tense. Those exchanges didn't go well, but his sons were forgiving. So was I. Just be aware how emotions can run wild. When we are tired, we don't always think our responses through. Sometimes our patience is as thin as our energy.

- *Passages in Caregiving*, by Gail Sheehy, copyright 2010 by G. Merrit Corp., Harper Collins Publishers.

CHAPTER 7

A Time to Rest

Therefore do not worry about tomorrow, for tomorrow
will worry about itself. Each day has enough trouble
of its own.

--Matthew 6:34

There is a time for everything, and a season for every
activity under heaven ... a time to be born and a time
to die, ... a time to plant and a time to uproot ...

--Ecclesiastes 3:1-2

Just a respite

There were many hospital stays in the three years that I cared for
Gene. I was almost relieved when Gene was in the hospital because
my thought was, "Now I don't have to worry." I felt he was being
cared for by professionals who knew his care better than I knew it.
I was glad to get a good night's sleep because I didn't have the night

dialysis cycler humming right above my head or the worry about alarms going off. It actually seemed like a little mental vacation. I would find that there are so many reasons that concept is not a true one.

Life for your loved one continues. He may have a bad night. She may experience fear, a bad reaction to medication, or any number of health problems. Once when I was casually entering Gene's room, I found his bed elevated to its highest position and several nurses around him. They had called in his nephrologist. I asked the doctor what was going on, and he said he didn't know. I may have had an eight- hour respite, but I still needed to know what had happened. Why was Gene so confused, and why did he seem overmedicated as the morning progressed?

Stay informed about your loved one's condition. Don't be afraid to ask the nurse what happened through the night or while you were not there. This is not just to empower you, but also to empower your loved one as much as you can.

Education is power even at this level. The more you know and the more informed questions you can ask, the better off you will both be. There may be little that can actually be done that will improve the situation, but whatever you can do to keep from feeling victimized is all to the good. The more involved and informed your loved one is, the less likely he/she will feel helpless and needy. I found that Gene was fearful much of the time when I was away. If the patient feels informed, the time away from you will not make him feel so insecure.

Enjoy a good night's sleep. Casually enjoy a cup of coffee and the news in the morning. Take your morning run or walk without the added worry and enjoy the fresh air. Then, as you enter the hospital, take a deep breath and get back to your life with your loved one, informed and supportive.

Addressing insecurities

Helplessness and neediness are common feelings for those who are feeling ill. We should not contribute to those painful emotions by not including them in decisions and ideas. Gene was not happy about being told what to do all the time. That led him to refuse some medications and therapy. All the appointments and changes in medication seem overwhelming to the caregiver. They may seem even more overwhelming to the one who is ill, especially when the patient doesn't feel any better from taking the medication. As long as patients can participate, include them in all conversations.

I know it is simpler and quicker just to talk medical treatment over with doctors or family members without including the one who is ill. In the long run, however, including the patient in the discussion can contribute to household peace. Letting Gene talk with the doctors, even when he was not fully coherent, would make him feel he had some sort of control over his treatment because he was included. Speaking with him, the doctors learned about his apprehension and the reasons for his resistance.

Maybe Gene didn't fully understand the need for some tests, and those questions or concerns are best addressed to the doctor or nurses. I didn't always know why certain tests were being done. We don't have all the answers, and asking questions together is good.

One of my clients has multiple sclerosis. She has had many complications and symptoms. As the symptoms arose, we always came up with reasons she was itching or her ankles would swell or she couldn't sleep. These seemed like conditions that could happen to anyone. We would try different lotions for her skin, encourage her to drink more water and keep her feet up, or suggest that she only drink decaf coffee. At an appointment with her neurologist, she told him about all her problems and wondered what she could do. He told her that every complaint she had was a symptom of her condition, multiple sclerosis. Even though there was nothing she could do about those symptoms, she was at peace, knowing that her symptoms were normal for her condition. I encourage you and your loved one to speak up and ask questions. Know as much as you can about the illness you are managing.

One of my clients felt insecure if her daughter, her husband, and I were talking and she was not a part of the conversation. She was sure we were talking about her in a negative way. If we talked about her care in front of her, she was upset because we were talking about her in her presence. You can see the dilemma. We finally had to explain that it is always important for those who work together to communicate with each other. We three were working together to make sure she had the best care. Although we would have to use her name to converse effectively, we were not talking about her behind her back or as though she was not there. If you have a helper from an agency, be aware of the insecurities and actions that may cause them.

We want to make everything "just so" for our loved ones, but they need to do as much as they can for themselves. There is a balance between helping people and making them feel dependent. The occupational therapist's job is to teach your loved ones how to do their own care as much as they can. Physical therapy generally gives them some exercises they can do on their own. Encourage them to do these exercises.

As therapy for her fine motor skills, one of my clients was supposed to color pictures and practice handwriting by tracing cursive letters like the ones we traced in second grade. She was okay with doing these exercises at first. Then she started to feel like a child. If I sat and did the exercises with her, she was much more likely to do them. It is hard to do tasks that seem so childish at a time in one's life when that person has already accomplished so much in a career or family.

Sometimes exercises like the ones mentioned seem easy to us. We may think we can accomplish something of our own as they are working on their exercises. They are called exercises because they are not easy for them. The exercises are a struggle, and the patients need encouragement to stay involved. It is always easier to stick with any exercise program if we have an accountability partner. Consider being that partner for your loved one.

The more you allow your loved ones to do for themselves, the more independent they feel. This truth applies even if the new way of doing a task is awkward and slow. There is dignity in doing it. It is okay for them to struggle a little to accomplish a task. Keep positive and help your loved one stay positive about the new venture. You may need to look at the situation clinically. Don't step in when you see them struggling; allow them to try and to accomplish a task. Of course there is no need to be cruel; sometimes it is good to offer a little help so they don't get too frustrated and want to give up. You will know those times as they arise.

Most hospitals have a home health equipment store near them. I found it a good idea to visit one and look around at all the different resources. I was unaware of all that was offered. Someone in the home health store is sure to offer you help or answer your questions. They have everything from walkers to electronic lifts to help with daily activities. Most medical equipment can be covered, to some extent, by Medicare or other insurances. The staff is generally on call 24/7 and can assist you if there is a problem with the equipment you purchase from them.

Even if you have no need for such equipment immediately, a walk through the store and a talk with a salesperson about your situation and fears can help. Just knowing what equipment is available can ease your fear.

Facing the end

As Gene neared three years on dialysis, his body chemistry became more and more imbalanced. So many symptoms started needing medical attention. We were making an emergency run to the hospital every two weeks. Sometimes they found something they could help, and sometimes none of the tests helped the doctors. Gene was extremely frustrated with the whole medical field, which was certainly understandable. There were a lot of tests and repeat tests. Perhaps if we had asked the doctor or a nurse to explain the tests, it would have helped Gene accept what was happening. As I said, we will question our decisions forever.

I would have probably just gone to bed or sat down if I had all the health problems Gene had. He was far braver than I am. Maybe it was because most of his life had been spent in an office alone, being his workaholic self. Gene, for whatever reason, wanted to live life until the end. I think he finally figured out all the living and relational truths he had been missing. He wanted to be with me— even if he had to sit on a bench while I did the shopping or sit in the food court at the mall while I browsed just to have a little personal time. We would have lunch and talk, and that made good memories.

It was important to Gene to visit his children even though getting him into the house was a chore at their house and later at ours. Getting out of the house was as good for him mentally as it was for me, and the time together and with family made good memories.

Gene loved a certain gospel group, the Gaither Vocal Band. The Gaither's recording studio and family center, which included a restaurant, gift shop, bookstore, and viewing of Gaither Homecoming DVDs, was only two hours away. A trip there was a great getaway for us to enjoy together, and often we took friends or family. It was a good day trip that didn't entirely wear Gene out. In fact, it was refreshing for both of us. There are usually brochures for local attractions at a hotel. Maybe you can find a fun place to get away with your loved one that would work for you. I know that once, when Gene was still fairly healthy, he suggested going up to the toll road nearby and looking at brochures. We had a great day doing something close by, and we had not known that pleasure existed until then.

I know that getting out for little dates was important to him. One morning it was raining, and I wanted to go out for breakfast. I always think breakfast out on a rainy day is romantic. He said he would go. Everything went pretty well until we got up to leave the restaurant after breakfast. I headed for the door and turned to check behind to see how he was doing. He was holding tightly to a chair and starting to fall. I caught him before he fell, and I suggested we go back to the booth, but he wanted to go home. He was determined to go out to the car. It took three male customers and me to get him to the car. Even so, it was hard. The owner of the restaurant asked me if he should call 911 so the paramedics could check him out right there in our car. I said yes, but Gene said no. I finally convinced Gene to let the paramedics come and check him out since it was free. I stalled as much as I could, and finally the paramedics arrived.

Gene was weak, and his breathing was shallow. His blood pressure had dropped to 95/70. Gene was really angry and determined, and still his blood pressure was that low. The paramedics suggested that he go to the hospital. Gene refused. I called the CAPD nurses, and they encouraged him to go, but he refused. The paramedics called the emergency doctor at the hospital, and he strongly suggested Gene go, but he refused. I called his son, and he begged his dad to go, but Gene refused. So I drove him home. Then he wanted to stay in bed. I doubt that he had felt well before we went out, but he liked our little dates.

Two days later he complained about the worse headache he had ever had, and he thought he needed to go to the chiropractor. I did not want to take him because I didn't know how we would ever get him into the office. He was too heavy for me to support if he became light-headed again, and this seemed far more serious to me than the kind of problem a simple adjustment would solve. God is good! Our chiropractor was on vacation. Gene was willing to go to the hospital, but he wanted me to drive rather than calling an ambulance. The hospital was an hour away. Halfway to the hospital, Gene said he didn't think he would make it.

By the time we got to the emergency room door, he was covered in sweat and totally unable to help the emergency aide and me to get him into a wheelchair. The nurses ran to him with a blood pressure cuff. His blood pressure was 268/110. They wheeled him to a room and said they would call me when he was settled. Soon I could go to his room in the ER. Doctors and nurses were everywhere. I sat in a dark corner out of the way, silent and stunned. One of the nurses asked me if there was anyone I could call to sit with me. I just looked at him and shook my head. I was exhausted from worry and activity. The last thing I wanted was to worry about someone else … directing them to the restroom or having them want to go to lunch or hold a conversation. I just wanted to sit there and stare and have my own thoughts.

A short man with a white suit and a goatee came in Gene's room. This sight caught my attention. I was told that he was a neurologist— the best, they said. He looked like Colonel Sanders to me, but that thought didn't even make me smile. I was numb. He looked at the scan they had done and other vitals and observations by the nurses and emergency room doctor. He walked over to me, and I stood.

"This is very serious … very serious."

"How serious is *very serious?*"

Not wanting to alarm Gene, he made a gesture. He whispered to me that Gene had a brain aneurism that had burst and bled on his brain stem. I backed away from him and returned to my seat to watch. The new information had sunk in, but I didn't know what to do with it. I still believed in miracles, and I was sure there would be one.

Gene always knew his name and birth date, who the current president was, and once they told him the day, he remembered that each time they asked. The nurse and Gene had a great conversation. After they were sure Gene was stable (and they didn't think that could happen under his circumstances), they took him to the ICU, where we both spent the night.

Gene never really recovered. For the next six weeks, we would talk to a number of doctors. He had procedures on his heart, physical therapy, occupational therapy, and speech therapy to help him recover again. He had lost all interest in food. He slept most of the day, and I begged God for answers about the reasons for all this suffering. His potassium had gotten too high. He had slipped into a coma during efforts to bring it down. Every time a doctor talked to him, Gene said he wanted to fight for his life, yet he could not sit on the side of the bed without assistance, and he made no effort to eat more than a bite or two of food.

Every day he became weaker and less interested in living. One day when I was sitting with him he told me, he had been awake most of the night and had made a decision. He had decided he did not want to live any longer.

When the physical therapists came in, he could not stand with them. They told me he was getting weaker each week. Speech therapists said that they were convinced that he would not ever be able to swallow enough food to sustain himself. The nurses were coming in every three days to pump his stomach because the mixture of nutrients they were pumping into his stomach at the lowest setting possible were not going on into his system. It did seem that life for Gene was over.

Every day might present more problems than we could cope with, but I hung onto hope. If nothing else, I just wanted to know what the purpose of his suffering was. I don't know that I hoped for a miracle; I just wanted some answers that would help me understand the purpose of all this suffering.

As I sat outside the ICU, one of the many times Gene had been there in the last few weeks, there was a family in the waiting area. Their husband and father had suffered a brain hemorrhage, and he was dying. I talked to one of the daughters and told her that I understood it was hard, but my husband had survived a brain bleed and had come out of it, but he was never the same and never would be. I suggested that maybe her father's passing was the best thing that could happen to him. She understood.

Gene wanted to stop all medications, be disconnected from the dialysis contraption near his bed, and come home to die. I understood what he wanted, and I certainly understood why. However, he had told his sons that he wanted to fight for life. I wanted him to talk to a nephrologist whom he trusted. We had seen many nephrologists, good and bad. I wanted to make sure that a reliable nephrologist felt there was nothing that could be done to make Gene's condition better. If his nephrologist said there was no real hope, then he needed to call his children together and let them know his decision. His children had been told earlier that he wanted to live and was willing to fight for life. Then I had also added to the deception unwittingly with my hopeful emails.

His nephrologist told us that if Gene continued as he was, he might have a year to live. Even if they put a permanent feeding tube into his stomach, and if he was able to survive that surgery and the one needed to change his dialysis port, (and that was very optimistic), he would need constant care in a nursing home.

That was all Gene needed to hear, and he yelled, "Disconnect me!"

I suggested that we could bring him home and call Hospice Care for help. I also wanted him to face his children and tell them his decision. He was willing. I asked the nephrologist what we could expect to happen in the days following his disconnection from dialysis. He said that Gene would have two weeks to live. I'm not sure why he said that because that is not what anyone else told us. At some point, the toxins in his body would reach his brain. At that point, Gene would "act like a drunken sailor." I had no idea what that meant, but I had a picture in my mind. Then he would be pain-free until he died, maybe a day later. I looked at Gene.

"I am ready to die. Disconnect me."

His daughter had come home every weekend to spend time with her dad. She sat quietly in a chair nearby as the doctor told us this prognosis. I looked at her helplessly.

"I'll call the family," she said as she got up from her chair.

I looked back at the doctor, who was looking at me. "Do you have any more questions?"

I shook my head and looked back at Gene. The evening was difficult, to say the least. I had spent the night at the hospital the night before, and I was exhausted. Gene wanted to be disconnected that very minute from the dialysis contraption. I asked him to stay connected until the next day, when they would make their normal exchange. I wanted him to have a few hours to think about his decision after he talked to his kids. One of his sons stayed the night with him. The next day, the nurse disconnected him and told me he had no more than five days to live. Gene's sister said that their uncle died three days after he stopped dialysis.

Surrounded by friends

I called Gene's best friend to let him know we were bringing Gene home. He arranged for our Sunday school class to come over and sing and have communion with him one last time.

Our Bible study leader arranged for our study group to come over and have Bible study with Gene one last time. They celebrated communion the night after our Sunday school class was there. It was an amazing fellowship both nights.

The toxins hit Gene's brain his first day home. By evening he was unable to move anything but his eyes. He was aware of our class being there that night, and he heard the songs we were singing. His eyes started to move back and forth quickly.

"What do you see?"

His speech was very weak and slurred, but I am positive he said, "Angels."

I put a tiny piece of bread dipped in juice on Gene's tongue as our pastor served communion. Gene was startled by the taste on his tongue.

"The Body and the Blood of Christ given for you," our pastor whispered.

Our pastor's wife, Anita, spent the night with me, and I cannot express how glad I was to have her there. At one point in the wee hours of the morning, Gene started to gag on the feeding tube still in his throat. The Hospice nurse and I had talked about the danger if such a thing should happen. She told me to go ahead and pull it if he did choke. I will never forget the helpless look in his eyes and the realization that he was utterly and totally dependent on me at that moment. He was unable to move anything except his eyes, and yet he needed to fight for his life because he was choking. The look was haunting to me, and I was so glad for the company of a friend.

The next day was quiet. I played some of his favorite DVDs of *Gaither Homecomings*. Anita stayed the next day with me because she believed he would die that day and didn't want me to stay alone. We bathed him and combed his hair, and I gave him a foot rub and a back rub.

That evening, as scheduled, the Bible study group came. Our leader told Gene who was there and why they were there. It wasn't until months later I realized how amazing this next gesture was. Gene lifted his arm in the air and moved it from one side to the other as if waving. He had not been able to move anything but his eyes since the toxins hit his brain. Our leader, Tim, asked us to open our Bibles to 1 Corinthians 15:35. He started reading, "How are the dead raised? With what kind of body will they come?"

The phone rang, and I went to answer it. When I returned to my seat, I didn't think Gene was breathing anymore. I watched for a while to make sure and also because I didn't want to believe that he might be dead. When I was certain he was not breathing, I went to his bed to check for a pulse, and there was none. Tim came and took Gene's wrist from my hand as tears were forming in my eyes. He checked his wrist for a pulse, and I checked at Gene's neck, but there was no pulse.

I felt so blessed to be surrounded by friends who cared so deeply about us that they would be there with us that night. Tim called the hospice nurse, and I called the family.

My caregiving days were over, and although I was familiar with grief from the many times Gene and I had tasted from its bitter cup during the last three years, its clutches were not welcome; its coldness felt intense. The rest I had longed for many times did not seem so sweet.

The Rest

The rest, I longed for
Not so long ago
Feels like a hollow heart.
Echoes of demands
Sound sweet now.
I check the bed,
But no one is there
I check the chair
Tears fall.
It is here
That rest
I longed to savor,
To enjoy and embrace,
Uninterrupted, timeless,
But now it clutches me and

It's cold …

EPILOGUE

The subject of grief is not one I'm going into here. Having attended two grief support groups, I find I am not the average griever. I'm not sure why. My best guess is that it's because I lost three key people in my life by the time I was seven and a half years old. My grandfather died; a little over a year later, my mother and younger brother were killed in a car accident. Possibly because I was a child and had the faith of a child, my view of life and death was very simple. I was able to find comfort in knowing my loved ones were with Jesus.

To me, that would be the happiest place to be, and I was happy for them. So, they were there, the happiest place ever, and I was here. I knew I would see them again, and I would pray to God to make their lives happy. That would be my simple way to stay in touch with them. I was still here, and I was happy in many ways—my life would go on. That was my simple way of handling grief. Childlike faith kept me trusting in his presence with them. If I wanted to give them a message, I would just pray to God to tell them. So I learned early to grieve simply.

At the very least, I learned that life goes on. It goes on differently, but it goes on. I do understand, however, that this truth is the worst thing you can say to someone who is grieving. We all grieve in our own ways and at our own pace. I don't think that my way of grieving is helpful for anyone, but it worked for me.

There are, however, some basic points that are the same for everyone. For instance, standing at the counter to eat meals instead of sitting at the table as you always did is common. There will be times when you think you are going crazy, but you are not. You may feel that there is a hole in your life and your heart that will never heal. Truthfully, that hole may or may not heal; that is up to you.

I had many bouts with depression over the years of my life. At some point, I got really tired of being depressed and even angry at the feeling. So, whatever it took, I would fight to get out of the depression. Grief felt like depression to me. It was heavy and lonely and a burden. It was not a place I wanted to be, but neither did I want to suppress it. I chose to feel it's every affect..

I told my friends and those in my grief group, "One year and I'm out. I will give myself one year. I will feel my grief to its very depths for one year, and then I am out."

Of course, during the process of caregiving for my husband, there had been several stages of grief already, and maybe that helped me. When someone loses their loved one totally unexpectedly, there is much more grieving to be done. It is important to take the time you need and not rush it.

The morning after Gene died, a friend came to spend the day with me. She did not know he had died. I was so glad to see her. We talked, and she let me tell her the details of the evening without interruption. After we had talked a while, she wondered if I would like to go out to lunch.

"That would be great," I said, "but I don't want to go anywhere in town because I don't want anyone to ask me how Gene is and then have to tell them he died."

"That's a good idea. Let's just drive around and look at life."

That was the most amazing realization. I had not realized how watching someone deteriorate and face death had made me forget about life. The flowers seemed so amazing. The colors were so bright in the warm sun. The grass was so green, and it was growing, and someone was mowing a lawn. It seemed so fresh. We drove by a golf course, and there was a grandfather, maybe even a great-grandfather, who was teaching his great-grandson to play golf. My friend stopped the car, and we watched as life was happening right in front of our eyes.

"I forgot," I said with a sort of wonder. "I forgot about life, about great-grandfathers and great-grandsons playing. I forgot about it all."

Other lives had progressed as I was trying hard to make Gene's life the best it could be, juggling family members' emotions, and trying to keep up with the tasks I needed to do at the house. I had actually been planning Gene's funeral during my drive to the hospital each morning with my coffee, with an extra shot of espresso, in one hand. My drive home had consisted of recounting the events of the day and wondering how I could help Gene be stronger or happier. I would have been wondering if I should have done something differently. Did I really understand what was going on with Gene? Should I have insisted on further treatment or another specialist?

All the time I was driving by Little League fields filled with children and families and life. I was passing families going to the beach or the zoo, and I was consumed by the thoughts of death and dying.

Now, as we were driving around, I was seeing husbands and wives on bicycle rides or walking hand in hand, and it was surreal that other people were happy and their lives were going on. I felt as if mine had ended.

Someone asked me to breakfast or lunch every day, and I sat there as though I was an observer with only one story to tell: "This is how he died."

At that time, Dish TV featured *Golden Girls* marathons. I would sit and watch those every time they were on. I think it was because they made me laugh out loud, and the sound surprised me. I couldn't remember when I had honestly laughed out loud. Laughing because something just struck me as funny was addictive. I became obsessed with *The Golden Girls* for about two years. I think my son was worried.

I would sometimes do things that would make me feel the pain. Feeling the pain of Gene's absence actually made me feel close to him. I would play songs we enjoyed and go places we had gone. I don't know if that is a good tactic.

The worst task was getting rid of all the dialysis supplies. The supplier would not take the bags of fluid back. I had to slit each bag, let it drain out, and then dispose of the bags. The boxes of fluid were heavy. Stabbing the knife into the bags was therapeutic, but nothing helped me see the hole in my life as much as disposing of the supplies. For the last three years, Gene's life and my life were both centered around his dialysis schedule. My time was consumed with knowing which strength of solution to use and hoping he did not have a cloudy drain bag, which would be the sign of infection. Keeping track of supplies and making sure we were home when the new supplies arrived had been vital.

I had tried to arrange the boxes of fluid so that they were a useful element of our furnishings, not an interruptive part of our house décor. How many times had I moved those boxes to keep our house from looking so much like a medical clinic? Those supplies represented a huge part of our lives those last three years, and now I was disposing of them as though they were nothing. I felt as if I was destroying and disposing of our life together. I had to remind myself that there was no life together anymore. In disposing of all those bags of fluid, I saw how big the hole in my life was, a hole that needed to heal. I had asked for help, but it was not a good time for anyone to come to help. I was truly glad I was alone. I needed to see the hole in my life. I needed to know and face its parameters. It was exhausting physically, mentally, and emotionally. But there was a *Golden Girls* marathon on that night.

There were words to songs I had never heard before, and suddenly they had a lot of meaning. Because Gene and I were such big Gaither fans, we had a lot of CDs and Homecoming DVDs. The Gaithers are gospel singers and have launched many Christian artists' careers.

There were songs on CD's that we owned I had listened to many times and had not really heard the words. I would listen to those CD's on my way to work and suddenly they seemed so appropriate for my day. I would listen to those songs and sob, sometimes all the way to work, once I got a job. My eyes must have been red and swollen from crying, but no one ever said a word. My first New Year's Eve was spent driving alone to an airport an hour away, on a snowy, windy night, to pick up my son.

"This is my life now," I sobbed.

I stared out at the lonely, cold night, hoping I would not slide off the road. The snow was blowing and making it very hard to see the road ahead. The snow plows had been out, but they could not stay ahead of the blowing snow. Driving along and watching signs in the blowing snow, I knew my exit was coming soon, but I missed it. The plows had piled snow at the turnoff, and that made it hard to tell the exit lane from the rest of the road. I felt so alone. The vastness of the white snow looked like another blank page in my life. I was afraid, but I was even more determined to make life work for me. This experience would be the first of many new challenges I would face.

How I grieved the loss of my husband is not for everyone, but it worked for me. It worked for me to stay determined every time I encountered something new. I found, after three months of being consumed with self-pity, that it was important to start thinking about helping others. Even if I only helped others in small ways, my focus changed. I started taking notice of the prayer requests at church and praying for those in need. Praying for others helped me feel connected with those who were hurting too. Spending time in the presence of God was as healing for me. But spending time with God to accomplish a purpose was better. I started knitting sweaters for children in orphanages again. I also knitted children's socks for a local charity. These simple activities helped me to refocus and think of others.

Although I considered myself a seasoned griever, there were still times I felt I would drown in my own grief and tears. One woman in a grief support group that I attended said she had been attending for five years after her husband died. She just couldn't move past his absence. A friend of mine, who had lost her husband four years prior, said that it takes at least three years to feel normal again. I was determined that I would be out of the grieving process in one year, but that is not exactly what happened. Of course we never forget our loved one or stop missing them. We must make our new normalcy in our own time. When we are ready to take any step forward, it must be at our own pace.

Printed in the United States
By Bookmasters